Brooklyn Existentialism:
Voices from the Stoop explaining how Philosophical Realism can bring about the Restoration of Character, Intelligence and Taste

Brooklyn Existentialism:
Voices from the Stoop explaining how Philosophical Realism can bring about the Restoration of Character, Intelligence, and Taste

Arthur DiClementi & Nino Langiulli

Fidelity Press
South Bend, Indiana
2008

Manufactured in the United States of America

1 2 3 4 5 6 10 09 08 07 06 05 04

Library of Congress Cataloguing in Publication Data

DiClementi, Arthur and Langiulli, Nino
       Brooklyn Existentialism: Voices from the Stoop
         p. cm.
       Includes bibliographical references and index
       ISBN 0-929891-06-6
       1. Philosophy. 2. Art. 3. Science. 4. Education.

TABLE OF CONTENTS

INTRODUCTION

The madness of our time is intoxicating. First it attracts, then it excites, but then it abandons, leaving behind relics of desperation. It is objective not subjective. This means that it is not the mental disease of particular individuals, although it is also that.

Rather, the madness infects the mind of the culture itself by virtue of the culture's ruling ideas. It is a madness that is omnipresent as it moves through the system of the world in the way a virus moves through an organism. It does so by virtue of the electronic technology of communication. This is a fact and not the whine of a luddite. Technology and communication are good things, not in themselves, but in their use and purpose which can be for bad intentions as well as good ones: good ones as educating in truth, goodness, and beauty; bad ones as indoctrinating in falsity, evil, and ugliness, which do indeed have their charm. Technology and communication are not gods, although the madness tries to make them so. Leaving things alone and silence are good things too; a truth ignored by the culture's elite. There is nothing about technology and communication that dissuades the seducers, i.e. the culture's elite, from turning the moral neutrality of technology and communication into moral excrement. Their success, however, depends upon the demonic charms of the seducers and the willing cooperation of the seduced for whom no temptation is so vile as to be resisted. Doesn't education consist in knowing what to resist as well as what to pursue? The long march of radical democratization and the accompanying decline of manners in speech, courtesy in behavior, and propriety in dress (Oh, that cruel tie!) together with the rise of vulgarity has led the seduced to imagine themselves as independent and unique. On one hand they think that they are victimized by various kinds of discrimination; on the other hand they willingly and madly embrace the bad ideas by which they are seduced; such as, their conviction that manners are inauthentic and oppressive. Their seduction by "the culture of cool" makes them incapable of being surprised by joy. In their willing embrace the seduced believe that they are the masters of their destiny. They do not know that they are seduced, and they do not know that they are mad. Should they get an inkling of their own fallibility, the god 'within' them cannot help, since that god is none other than themselves ruled by pleasure and wishful thinking driven to excess. If, by some chance however, pleasure turns into pain, then there is hope. For then they may begin to hear voices other than the voices from within. If they still have ears to hear those voices whose sound echoes the past, then those voices will be speaking the language of existentialism, with a Brooklyn dialect and accent.

Why Existentialism? Why the variant from Brooklyn? Because what we are calling Brooklyn Existentialism is the effort to restore the practical and theoretical wisdom of the Hebrews, Greeks and Romans as synthesized in Christianity. This is to say that, speaking poetically, Brooklyn Existentialism is both tragic and comic; for it recognizes both the death of the God–Man — the paradigm of tragedy — and His resurrection — the paradigm of comedy. The comic hero overcomes the dramatic conflict by which the tragic hero destroys himself and destroys others. As the existentialism from Brooklyn, our account will treat the ruling bad ideas with dismissive ridicule.

In other words, human existence is existence-in-the-world, not as a hypothetical disinterested spectator but as an engaged actor. Brooklyn Existentialism leaves the hypothetical and disinterested spectator in the shadows of modern philosophy to ruminate at the margins of knowledge and practice. As existence-in-the-world, human existence is contingent in all respects — in the domain of knowledge, in those of morality and politics, and in those of art and aesthetics. Human beings have access to all these domains and can achieve success in them. Or what then is hope for? They can also fail and fail completely. Or what then is hell for? To recognize and acknowledge human mortality or human finitude is the same as recognizing and acknowledging human contingency and the contingency of everything else in creation.

The voices from the Brooklyn stoops (a Dutch word from Dutch Brooklyn as is the word Brooklyn, *Breukelen*, itself) affirm the critical common sense realism of Western pre-modern philosophy. They also confirm Existentialism's return, for the most part, to pre-modern thought's emphasis on the ontological priority in contrast to modern thought's emphasis on the epistemological priority. This means that Brooklyn Existentialism starts with the fact that something exists and the question of what it is, rather than the questions of whether or not we can know what exists and how we know it. Brooklyn Existentialism eschews the latter as the beginning of sophistry — the musings of the philosophical "smart-aleck." It affirms rather the combination of street wisdom and traditional thought. It defends morality without being moralistic, Self-righteous indignation permeates the Civil Rights movement, the Feminist movement, and the Gay Rights movement, the Peace movement, and the Environmentalist movement. For example, opposition to government coerced affirmative action *ipso facto* entails for such moralists racism, sexism, and homophobia. Private affirmative action is another matter. That happened in Brooklyn in 1947 when the Dodgers hired Jackie Robinson to play baseball for them and the people of Brooklyn – an excellent example of what Christian philosophers call the common good. Through that action the Dodgers showed themselves to be not only Brooklyn's team but the authentic "America's team."

Government coerced affirmative action led to the public name-calling which replaced morality understood as telling the truth, keeping one's promises, and loyalty to God, family, and country. This name-calling and the moralistic sophistry which drives it masks the fact that lying, cheating, and stealing are immoral actions whereas racism, sexism, and homophobia are not actions at all but are attitudes which may or may not lead to immoral action. These voyages into sophistry are passports to skepticism, cynicism, solipsism and nihilism. Such sophistry, which when blessed by moralistic intentions, coupled with public policy preferences are difficult if not impossible to check.

Brooklyn Existentialism is blunt, brash, sometimes rude but without pretense and affectation. Because it is traditional, it is suspicious of fads and dismissive of cant of any kind. It is unashamedly "judgmental." For Brooklyn Existentialists make judgments as everyone does and must with respect to everything and anything. Judging hastily is what it hopes to avoid. That is what common sense exhorts. That is what Brooklyn Existentialism as claptrap detector commands. As far as the idea of Brooklyn "tough-guys" is concerned, it is to be dismissed as just another pretense. The 19th century Texas Rangers were tough guys. US Navy Seals and British Commandos are tough guys. Furthermore, tough guys are to be found nearly everywhere on earth, as, for example, the Gurkhas from Nepal. Not only Brooklyn Existentialists, but reasonable people would find a bit of California dreaming in New York Senator Charles Schumer's claiming recently (April 2005) in Washington D.C. that since he is from Brooklyn, "[he] likes a fight." The toughness we speak of here is toughness of thought with a Brooklyn accent. This is less so of contemporary Brooklyn. Rather it is the toughness of Great Depression Brooklyn, World War II Brooklyn, Fifties Brooklyn – that era when "Brooklyn was the world" for Brooklynites – that era when its culture was a confluence of those of the Jews, the Irish, the Blacks, the Italians and the Poles. English and Dutch Brooklyn was of an earlier time in its history when it was the Protestant Brooklyn of Horace Greeley and Henry Ward Beecher.   Even then Brooklynites proudly differentiated themselves from New Yorkers, i.e., Manhattanites. This is evident from the resistance on the part of Brooklynites to Brooklyn's incorporation into greater New York.

This toughness of thought is another name for the critical common sense realism we mentioned earlier. It will be applied throughout our considerations not only to the practical everyday actions in the madness of our time but also to the theoretical foolishness in mathematics, the physical sciences, and philosophy. It will be applied especially to the behavioral sciences as performed by those three stars of Modern *and* Postmodern fictional science — Charles Darwin, Karl Marx, and Sigmund Freud. Friedrich Nietzsche gets honorable mention as best supporting actor. The smart-alecks need not remind us that Darwinism does not fit neatly into the behavioral sciences but social Darwinism (as the inefficacy of the unfit) does; and Darwin's theory (viz. natural selection through gradual random variations as the mechanism for the efficacy of the fit) does not fit quite so neatly into empirical biology either. As for Marx and Freud, even the smart-alecks can no longer promote them. Both claimed that their theories were scientific, but the theories were not. It is difficult to think of a single Marxian doctrine that is true or practice that is right. For example, the ideas of economic determinism, the alienating nature of private property, class warfare, the inevitable march of history toward a classless society and the inevitable collapse of liberal capitalism are not true; while socialist planned economics and coerced redistribution of wealth are not right or good.

In the face of such failure in theoretical and practical matters, dogmatic and fanatical Marxists want to give Marx "another chance." At Amherst College, for example, students are asked in a course whether Marxism still has credibility and whether societies can receive new insights into themselves by "returning to [Marx's] texts?" The course also claims that the actually existing Marxism of such mass murderers as Lenin, Stalin, Mao, and Pol Pot was a misapplication of Marxist ideas. Of course! And angels dance on the heads of pins. If, however, teachers and students want to study Marxism to find out how bad and false ideas can dominate the intellectual lives of people over a century, then they should. Education consists not only in knowing what to pursue but also in knowing what to resist.

And whatever Freud said that is true, was not original. Whatever he said that was original, is not true. For example, what was original, such as the ideas of a universal Oedipus Complex, and of sexual repression as both the cause of neurosis and the cause of civilization are not true; while the importance of the erotic, dreams, the unconscious, and that of early childhood experience is not original. Plato, St. Augustine, and Nietzsche taught those ideas before Freud and more profoundly. Yet Freud continues to have his defenders. Too much of their intellectual capital was spent on promoting Freudianism as the explanation of everything from civilization to cigars. Even such a Yale literary guru as recently deceased Harold Bloom, while acknowledging that Freudianism is neither science nor medicine, wants to retain the study of Freud as literature and mythology because Freud possesses "cognitive insight, stylistic splendor [and] wisdom" ("Why Freud Matters," *Wall Street Journal.* 5/5/06, p. A16). "No," says critical common sense realism. What cognitive insight can there be in writing that expresses falsehood? Stylistic splendor compared to whom? Certainly not to Melville, Dickens, Hawthorne, Bernanos, Lampedusa, Faulkner. Kafka or Flannery O'Connor!

As for wisdom, how can there be any if it rests on falsehoods? There is so little time in our finite lives that we ought not to waste it on bad ideas and charlatanism. Now that's wisdom! The assertion of a universal Oedipus Complex in human beings is not. Freud's legion of apologists summarily dismiss any challenge or criticism, and they have been doing this for decades. Their defense typically accuses challengers of resorting to *ad hominem* attacks while ignoring the legitimate arguments presented as criticisms. Critical common sense realists can only wonder if Freud's protectors even know what an *ad hominem* argument is. To illustrate, if one were to characterize Freud as a phobia-ridden cocaine addict who banged his sister-in-law, destroyed their love letters and denied the seduction, then supporters would be justified in their complaint. That's an *ad hominem* argument!

Unlike Freud and Marx, Darwin was an authentic scientist. As a result, he gave scientific credibility to the Enlightenment ideals of "progress" and a "rationalism" detached from nature, that is to say, a disincarnate reason. The theory of Darwinian evolution, however, has not adequately met the challenges advanced by its critics; rather, those challenges have been dogmatically dismissed. The theory claims that life came from inanimate matter as a result of random events. How do they know the events were random? Is that science, supposition or, dare we suggest, dogma? "Randomness" or, as some others call it, "chaos" has never been experienced by anybody. Randomness in Darwinian evolution is a metaphysical concept and does not qualify as a scientific hypothesis. Disorder, often confused with randomness, has been experienced by everybody. Disorder is an affect based on the reality of order.

If evolution simply means adaptation within species or change over time then we agree that evolution is a "fact." But Darwinian evolution does much more than that. It claims to explain the origin of all living things through gradual "beneficial" changes occurring "randomly" and driven by "natural selection." Darwinian evolution means making new species and not simply changing what already exists. Simply put, reptiles evolved into birds and so on. If Darwinian biologists want to insist that "evolution is a fact," then we are entitled to ask, "Where is the evidence?"

When new species appear, we are told it's due to natural selection. When existing species become extinct, it's also due to natural selection. This is one hell of a theory. Real scientists and critical common sense realists ask: "How does one test such a 'theory'?" and "Given a specific species, is it on its way up or on its way out?"

The problems don't end there. Darwinian evolution claims that natural selection is the engine driving evolution. As a consequence, natural selection is making choices, *an act generally associated with intelligence and purpose,* and these choices are "beneficial" because they lead to the survival of the fittest. Using Spencer's formlatin of "survival of the fittest" for Darwin's "natural selection" raises the specter of circularity. Those living things which survive are the fittest. Which living things are the fittest? Those which survive. Logically, the argument is circular and says little about the origin of living things. Questions remain. Introducing the concept of adaptation only puts off the circularity. it does not eliminate it. What is the role of natural selection prior to organisms reaching the stage of reproduction, sexual or asexual? In the case of sexual reproduction, did males evolve before females, did females evolve before males, or did they evolve together?

Then every once in a while, we hear about the discovery of a missing link, i.e., an intermediate species. Recently the fossil of a "purported" extinct animal called Tiktaalik is supposed to provide the evolutionary missing link between bony fish and land-dwelling vertebrates. Tiktaalik is also supposed to provide an answer to critics of Darwinism who argue that the absence of intermediate species damages the theory. Darwinists claim that the gaps in the current explanatory model have a Tiktaalik waiting to fill it. In fact, the "purported" missing link between reptiles and birds (Archaeopteryx) is still being presented in high school and college textbooks in biology. We use the word "purported" here deliberately because a similar enthusiastic faith was vested in the Coelacanth fossil. Darwinists assured us that it was a missing link until 1938 when a living Coelacanth was discovered in the Indian Ocean. Darwinists were unperturbed and unapologetic when they found out that their extinct Coelacanth turned out to be extant. The gang on the stoop is holding back on the giggles over the thought of a "living fossil," an oxymoron which diminishes the meaning of both words.

Here are some questions from the stoop. Is Tiktaalik extinct? Will it cease to be extinct when a living specimen is caught? What does extinct mean in the Darwinian lexicon? How do Darwinists know that Tiktaalik is an intermediate species or transitional form between bony fish and vertebrates, and not another distinct and independent species? The same doubts can be raised over the "Indonesian Hobbit" (*Spiegel Online International*, 9/01/06). Is the fossil a newly discovered small human being, or is it the skeleton of a prehistoric and intermediate species between primates and homo sapiens? And finally, are they shaving the corners of a square peg to force it in a round hole?

Scientific study in biology can be and is done without reference to Darwinism (Philip S. Skell, "Why Do We Invoke Darwin," *The Scientist*, August 29, 2005). There are biologists who ignore Darwinism in their studies and their teaching. These agnostics could and do cite as the model for their view and practice, geneticist Gregor Mendel, whose work owes nothing to Darwinism but which no one denies to be scientific. There is even a domain of current biological research called "cladistics" which restricts itself to taxonomy, i.e., describing, labeling, and classifying organisms much as Aristotle did. Darwinists bemoan this "return to Aristotle."

For critical common sense realism, the sciences must be scientific, not ideology or surrogate religion. Being scientific means observing, experimenting on, drawing inferences about and explaining nature, not projecting wishes and desires on her. The testing of hypotheses, moreover, is no excuse for an "anything goes" kind of science. It does not take geniuses to foresee the bad consequences of unrestrained testing in the belief that science is the holy inquisitor of all human problems. Practical wisdom must act as a limit to speculative science. What Clint Eastwood as Dirty Harry says in the movie *Magnum Force* (1973) applies particularly to scientists who conceive of science as the conquest of nature: "A man has got to know his limitations."

Marx, Freud, and Darwin, whatever their bad ideas are, held onto the concepts of meaning, truth, and causality. Nietzsche, however, whose ideas are not as well known or as influential as these others (except among intellectuals), is the primary philosopher of Postmodernism and Deconstructionism. His thoughts are more radical than the others because he *does* attack the concepts of rational discourse and scientific explanation, i.e., meaning, truth and causality.

Nietzsche understood well the rationalism of the Enlightenment, evaluated it, and carried it to its logical conclusion. His philosophy is both the culmination of modernity and its rejection. He uses the names of two Greek gods, Apollo and Dionysius, to refer to the dual character of nature and reality — Apollo standing for rationality and order, Dionysius for frenzy and disorder. At the basis of Western rationality and order lies frenzy and disorder. In order to find this out he says in *The Birth of Tragedy* that we must deconstruct, i.e., take apart, piece by piece, the structure of Western Civilization to discover that there is no rational foundation for it, only unreason and chaos (Ch.3). He also says this in his essay, *Truth and Falsity in Their Ultramoral Sense* (1872) by arguing that truth is "a mobile army of metaphors, metonymies, anthropo-morphisms," that "truths are illusions of which one has forgotten that they are illusions." In other words, there is no truth only fictions by which we ward off the absurdities and terrors of existence.

In the *Will to Power* (1901) he takes on "the principle of non-contra-diction" (the same thing cannot be and not be at the same time under the same circumstances), that is, the principle of meaningful discourse, and treats it too as a fiction. He says, "[A]ccording to Aristotle, the *principium contradictionis* is the most certain of all principles… the most ultimate of all and the basis of ev-ery demonstration." Nietzsche, however, regards the principle as an *imperative* — a command we give to nature to make her stand still so that we can control her. He says, that "logic would be an imperative, *not* directed at the knowledge of truth, but at the adjusting and fixing of a world *which must seem true to us*" (§ 516).

In the same *Will to Power*, he takes the principle of scientific explana-tion, i.e., the principle of causality (for every event, there is a cause) and treats it too as a fiction. He says, "We have absolutely no experience concerning *cause*; viewed psychologically we derive the whole concept from the subjective convic-tion that *we* ourselves are causes…" (§ 551). There is no such thing as a cause or an effect. The concept of causality is an illusion.

He accepts Darwinian evolution and endorses a morality that befits a nature that is, in Tennyson's words, "red in tooth and claw." That morality is not the moderation of Aristotelian ethics, not the moral law of the Mosaic code and especially not the Christian doctrine of love which he despises as a slave morality. It is, however, the warrior code, the martial ethics of the Homeric ep-ics as the master morality. It is this negation of Aristotle, Moses, and Jesus and affirmation of Homer that constitutes Nietzsche's "transvaluation of values."

Such poetry! Man, for Nietzsche, is the story-telling animal. But the stories are not written in verse and they do not rhyme (for those who think that poetry still has to rhyme). The voices from the stoop have a few questions for "Fast Freddie." Is it true that truth is an illusion? If so, then there is at least one truth that is not an illusion. What is a metaphor if all words are metaphors? Without the difference between literal words and metaphors, you couldn't know what a metaphor is. Is it true that Nazis committed genocide on the Jews? Or is that an illusion? Is it true that the earth revolves around the sun? Or is that an illusion? Is dissimulation simple falsehood or is it lying? How does one tell the difference? How could someone find out? Such questions presume, of course, that meaning, truth, and explanation are possible.

Since Freddie has told us that truth, the principle of non-contradiction and the principle of causality are fictions with which we keep big bad absurd and horrible nature at bay, what happens when we believe him and accept that they are just fictions? Taken as fictions, the ideas of truth, meaning, and explanation cannot do what they are intended to do, i.e., enable us to know, understand and explain.

If the martial values are the only true values and if the Christian doctrine of self-sacrifice, i.e., laying down one's life for one's friends is a slave morality, then Sergeant McChesney (Victor McLaglen) in *Gunga Din*, the movie, could never think: "You're a better man than I am, Gunga Din."

Brooklyn Existentialism is a premodern philosophy, as we said earlier, when we referred to the Classical thought of the Greeks and Romans, the Biblical religion of the Hebrews and their incorporation into Christian Theology. While it is ancient, it is not antiquated. Indeed it is trans-temporal. While it is the wisdom of Europe, it is trans-cultural and, at the same time, happily at home in Brooklyn.

Since, as we have already said, the madness of our time is a result of the culture's ruling ideas and since these ideas are an infectious disease, then we shall call them by their technical and scientific name – bad ideas.

Not negative ideas as the nonjudgmental smart-alecks would prefer it, but bad ideas – bad in practice because they are destructive and bad in theory because they are not true, not good (if we may be permitted a tautology for rhetorical reasons). The chapters of the book will be divided according to the bad ideas found in education, in the behavioral sciences, the physical sciences, in religion, the law, psychology, and the arts. Sociology, history, physics, mathematics and philosophy are subject matters studied in colleges and universities where the smart-alecks live and where, if they are not careful, minds go to die. Our methodology, you should pardon the expression, will be to announce the bad ideas and then subject them to a critical common sense realism expressed in ordinary language with a Brooklyn accent, i.e., the voices from the stoop.

Should anyone complain that our considerations are unscientific, we acknowledge the complaint and reply that we are self-consciously anecdotal as are participant observers in anthropological narratives. We are unashamedly anecdotal. Anecdotes contain their own truth and disclose the limitations of "scientific studies."

CHAPTER ONE:
The Madness in Education

The cultural battle lines are drawn at the school house door. Bad ideas assault the pursuit of the common good in the guise of innovative reform. Uncritical administrators, maleducated teachers, and a trusting public embrace these bad ideas in desperate hope that something will right the widespread failure that is public education. Whole language, new math, ethnomathematics, values clarification, holistic writing, and child-centered learning are just a few recent examples of the follies that have invaded and conquered schools, colleges, and universities. And this madness has been going on for some time, as anyone can find out from reading books such as *Left Back* by Diane Ravitch, a Texan currently from Brooklyn.

The nonsense and madness in current education begin with brainless ideas formulated as absolute disjunctions. Either this or that. If this, then not that; if that, then not this. Here are some examples: mechanical versus naturalistic learning, verbal versus hands-on, rote learning versus discovery, and lockstep versus individual developmentally appropriate instruction. This list is not exhaustive but it is sufficient to illustrate the point that reform in education is reduced to simplistic pairs of alternatives as the "innovative" breakthroughs are introduced. Educrats trumpet the ideas that children will fail in schools where the learning is mechanical, the instruction is traditional, and the progress is lockstep. They insist that children will blossom in classrooms and schools where the learning is naturalistic, the methods of instruction are "liberated" from subject content, and students' progress is to be self-paced. Education's "pitch-persons" guarantee parents that children will flourish "naturally" at their own pace in modern classrooms where traditional methods no longer prevail. But the facts are that students leave school illiterate, innumerate, and unintelligible. Educrats, bureaucrats, and politicians commercialize learning with such self-serving slogans as: "All children can learn," "No child left behind," "Every child on grade level." Cheerleading encourages and rewards the "reformers," while children are still left behind. They unbolted more than the desks when they freed students from the authority of both the teacher and traditional curricula.

Whole Language Theory and Learning to Read

The rhetoric of liberty masks the bad ideas. Whole language theory advances a false naturalism that dismisses the effectiveness of phonics; that is, learning words and sentences through their component sounds. It insinuates romantic ideology into the practical tasks of learning to read and learning to speak. Both learning to speak and learning to read are deliberate human endeavors. Remove deliberation and choice and you don't have human beings. Memory, repetition, habit and drill are not inimical to human nature. Simply put, knowing and caring about the difference between a period and a comma celebrate human behavior, and they renounce simian behavior. And if you reply, "Whatever," you should have your membership in the human race revoked.

Whole-language was indeed a "natural" for the schools of education, which insist that children are naturally motivated to learn and are not to be subjected to active and direct instruction. Any attempt to incorporate phonics into reading instruction was dismissed as traditionalist or conservative and its advocates as conspirators of the far right, according to gurus of whole language theory. *Ad hominem* salvos are no substitute for research, evidence, and reasoned argument.

Learning to read through a phonics approach is mindlessly identified with "conservative" traditional methods despite the evidence that reading instruction that includes phonics is the most effective method. Teaching phonics in the first two grades of primary school should be followed by a transition to edifying stories, and we don't mean dopey *Dick and Jane* books. Anybody with a library card knows that there are plenty of good stories around. Sensible people find this proposal compelling and they embrace a balanced approach combining phonics, comprehension, and stories that elevate the human spirit. But the "progressives" dismiss common sense, insisting that such an approach is simplistic and wrong headed. They continue to oppose instruction in phonics.

Utopian idealizations usually trump facts in the controversies concerning education. Whole-language in particular and progressive education in general err in believing that learning is automatic once utopian idealizations are served. Common sense realism shouts: screw the educrats; screw progressive education; and screw utopian idealizations. Set aside he romantic rhetoric and teach our children to read, write, and compute.

Yellow Buses — Yellow Peril

In American cities if you throw a rock in any direction from the street corner where you are standing, you will hit a public school. A child's day outside the home began with a short walk, often with others, to the neighborhood school. What do we have today? Yellow buses clog the city streets in the scramble to ensure "equal opportunity." What genius of social engineering thought this up? Think of garbage trucks and delivery trucks competing with yellow buses in the morning commute and you will understand the Byzantine complexity that is the bureaucratic management of public education. Rather than improve the neighborhood school (and we do know how to do it), we add unnecessary complexity, confusion, and expense. Utopian idealizations placate the bureaucrats and torment the public and the children. Can anyone think of a better metaphor, other than the lunatic asylum or a vision of hell, to represent the absurdity of contemporary American education than the yellow school buses on the city streets during the morning commute?

When children walk or skip to school, their arrival is as natural as walking to the corner grocery store to buy a loaf of bread. When children board yellow buses, they encounter harassment, cruelty, abuse, delays in traffic, lapses in security, bombs, and armed kidnappers. Can you see what's going on here! If you can't, then, buddy, you are a moron. Progressive attempts to fix the schools continue to worsen education and diminish civil society. Busing was a political solution to a problem in education, an artifact of progressive educators' desire to commingle politics with education. In those places where government enforced busing exists, it has failed. Busing, implemented to achieve equality in education, exacerbated differences in achievement and did little to improve the education of disadvantaged children. The most recent addition in the busing follies is found in New York City where the projected increase in school transportation costs is twenty-five million dollars. Since the schools now open at different times, the yellow buses must be rescheduled and deftly rerouted to get the children to school on time.

The Condom Conundrum

The child-centered theorists and the "inevitableists" argued relentlessly for a school policy to distribute condoms to the students. Advocates argued that children were having sex ever younger and encouraged them to use condoms, thus making irresponsible behavior "safe" as in "safe sex." Since it was inevitable that the students would have sex, condom distribution would make it safe.

Critics objected that condom distribution would sanction this irresponsible behavior and surreptitiously encourage students to engage in sex. This objection was dismissed on the "grounds" that students having sex was inevitable. Faculty "workshops" were scheduled to discuss the pros and cons of distributing condoms to students. Opponents of condom distribution argued that students were drinking alcohol ever younger. Since lunch is served daily, a martini should be included with lunch. By doing so, the school would encourage students to drink responsibly. Advocates for condom distribution shouted that drinking was different. Their ideological and fanatical commitment to

"condoms on demand" clouded their judgment, preventing them from concluding that underage drinking and underage sex are irresponsible behaviors. The
utopian idealists accept liberation through sex, but shun liberation through
intoxication. They took phonics out of the schools and put condoms in. The
irony is that many students cannot read the instructions on the package of
condoms. Safety precluded by illiteracy!

For those who insisted that condom distribution would not accelerate
the craving for pansexualism, we quote clinical psychologist, Dr. Joel Becker,
who addressed a group of Boulder High School students on April 10 at the
2007 Annual Conference of World Affairs (You can't make this stuff up!); "I'm
going to encourage you to have sex, and I'm going to encourage you to use drugs
appropriately. And why I am going to take that position is because you're going
to do it anyway."

Junior High Schools

The "experts" who advocated a differentiated curriculum did not limit
their influence to course content and pedagogy. The social engineers who di-
vined that many children would not be going to college believed that the responsibility of the school was to determine the right program for each child.
Children diverted from the academic curriculum were tracked into vocational
or commercial programs; which would have been okay if added to the traditional core curriculum in the arts and sciences. At the turn of the twentieth
century, junior high schools appeared. The common elementary course of
schooling was reduced from eight years to six. The original design of junior
high schools was intended to provide differentiated courses of study to prepare
students for their "place in society." Critics argued that this early curriculum
differentiation would promote social stratification and deny students access
to a common curriculum. With little evidence to support this current "fad,"
school officials throughout the nation, at great cost, reorganized elementary

schools and created junior high schools. The ladder of education extending from early childhood to college was replaced by differentiated paths leading to professional, commercial, vocational, agricultural or domestic destinations. An anti-intellectual educational determinism sorted students early and predetermined their futures. Not surprisingly, the appeal of junior high schools has waned and districts are returning to eighth grade elementary schools.

Social Studies

Ask the average college graduate to identify his elected representatives and you will understand the consequence of replacing history and geography with "social studies." This new "innovative" curriculum replaced the traditional course of study, which included ancient history, European history, geography, and American history. Experts, such as John Dewey and Charles Prosser, argued that the traditional four-year sequence was too academic and replaced it with "social studies." They reasoned that most students would not go on to college and insisted that students learn the skills and attitudes needed to take their place in society. The curriculum should be designed to meet the goals of "social efficiency." Proponents of the new "social studies" believed that the content of history should be based on the student's immediate interests. Ideological commitment to "child-centered" education crippled intelligence and common sense.

Antonio Gramsci, a Communist intellectual and critic of "natural" methods, warned that this "new" and "democratic" approach to education would be deleterious to the "oppressed." He argued that this new type of education would perpetuate class differences. Gramsci concluded that poor children, "flourishing naturally," would remain ignorant and would not rise above their social status and economic circumstances. The social efficiency movement advocated by "progressive" educators at the turn of the twentieth century implemented a "differentiated curriculum" that simply crystallized the status quo. It is ironic that the political partisans who champion the policies and practices of progressive educators fail to understand that the disparity between the "haves" and the "have-nots," recently characterized as "two Americas," can be attributed to the social engineering and social efficiency ideas implemented for over one hundred years.

Today, proponents of social studies advocate "multiculturalism" and "a curriculum of inclusion." These contemporary expressions of social studies do no more than cut students off from Western civilization's tradition rooted in ancient Greek philosophy, Roman law, and Judeo-Christian morality. Cut off from this tradition, students are set adrift on a sea of cultural relativism — a worldview that encourages them to satisfy their immediate desires and explore their narrow interests while dismissing the development of character, responsibility, and intelligence. Propaganda and indoctrination replace education.

Multiculturalism, Diversity, and Tolerance Revisited

Reasonable people knew that American education was headed down the corridor of bad ideas since it was directed by such documents as *The Cardinal Principles of Secondary Education* (1918). E. D. Hirsch, Jr., in his criticism of 20th century "reforms" of education entitled *The Schools We Need and Why We Don't Have Them* (1996), says:

> *Historians date the present era of American education from the publication in 1918 of Cardinal Principles of Secondary Education. Written by the Commission on the Reorganization of Secondary Education, and published by the Bureau of Education of the U.S. Department of the Interior, it was an official document that represented mainstream educational thought (p. 48).*

Two things stand out for the gang on the stoop after a century of this kind of "reform" stuff. First, it is a bureaucratic document trying to address the "felt" needs of the time. It ignored the fact that there already existed a history and tradition of education, both for those students who wished to pursue the academic life and for those students who wished to pursue the vocational life. There were universities for the former, and apprenticeships for the latter. If students went only to the eighth grade, they were supposed to be literate and numerate. Mechanics, electricians, plumbers, carpenters, and all others involved in the trades were required to have the ability to read, write, and calculate. These abilities are still required today. As far as literacy is concerned, the true test of it is not the ability to read but the ability to write. Remember Ken Burns' documentary on *The Civil War* (1990) and the letters written by the soldiers and their wives to each other? We're talking about enlisted men, not officers. Those letters were literate to the point that even current college professors could not write such letters.

Since 1918 there have been many documents from the educrats, and the ideas have gone from bad to worse. Just consider *The Portland* [Oregon] *Baseline Essays* of 1981, the New York State Board of Regents "Curriculum of Inclusion" of 1989 and its revision in 1991: *One Nation, Many Peoples: A Declaration of Cultural Interdependence*. In these curricula the issues were racial and ethnic as the substance of education presented under the banner of multiculturalism, a sophism if there ever was one. Culture is what societies have in common. Multi-racial and multi-ethnic societies are possible; a multi-cultural society is not. Diversity on its own cannot produce a society in common. Language, ideas, manners, and religion are examples of what unify societies. Examples of failed multicultural societies are Yugoslavia, Sri Lanka, the Basque section of Spain, Kashmir, and Jordan.

Wedded to the bad idea of multiculturalism, which is rooted in an absolutized idea of democracy (rule of the people without law) with its equally absolutized idea of equality (equal in one respect, i.e., human rights, then equal in all), are the absolutized ideas of diversity and tolerance. Diversity in practice in the U.S.A. is code for affirmative action for minorities and women in schools and in the workplace. What it should mean in a good society is diversity of ideas and diversity of talent, not diversity of race, sex, or ethnicity. Some products of diversity in the latter sense are such monstrosities as Ethnomathematics (mathematics based on race and ethnicity); Ebonics (non-standard English); Newtonian physics, dismissed as phallocentric, i.e., "masculine" physics; and equivalence of painting, sculpture and architecture. To say "diversity is our strength" is nonsense. When diversity fails, more tolerance is urged, more diversity.

Historically, the Moslem Arabs had the same information the Christian Europeans had, especially during the Middle Ages when they had more, but did not develop it into modern science. The Christians did so because that same information was culturally nested in such realities as hope, freedom, and a faith inseparable from reason and truth. Islam is fatalistic; therefore, no hope or freedom. Its faith is detached from reason and truth.

Tolerating *all* differences is illogical and impossible. It is illogical because intolerance cannot be tolerated. The intended consequences of the tolerance commissars are hate crimes and hate speech, for which there are now punishments. Tolerating the cuisine of cannibals is impossible; so too are the practices human sacrifice and mutilation of the sex organs of women. Enforced tolerance and diversity lead to euphemisms, deceit, cynicism, and finally to nihilism.

The literature of tolerance and diversity is not only banal and mushy, but downright harmful. It invites destroyers to dinner. It attempts to destroy, in the name of tolerance, ordinary and normal human emotions and any possible thoughts of self-defense. Consider some "classics" in that literature such as Sara Bullard's *Teaching Tolerance: Raising Open-Minded Empathetic Children* (1996); Stern-LaRosa and Bettman's *Hate Hurts: How Children Learn and Unlearn Prejudice* (2000); and Mike Rose's "United We Stand: Schools Deliver Crucial Message on Tolerance," in *The American Teacher* (12/01-1/02). Rose's essay was written just after the attack on the Twin Towers and was meant to head off, and rightfully so, any anti-Arab thoughts or feelings at P.S. 261 in Brooklyn, where one in five students comes from an Arab family. But the intentions of the literature of tolerance go far beyond protecting innocent Arab children from their schoolmates. The intentions are to preach pacifism, to blur distinctions between friends and enemies, and to leave students unprepared to face their foes. We can be sure, moreover, that in the atmosphere of multiculturalism, diversity and tolerance, the students are not being taught about the heroism during World War II of the Marines at Guadalcanal in 1942 or that of the Paratroopers at Normandy in 1944.

The second thing that stands out is the use of the expression "mainstream educational thought." Keep your hand on your wallet when you hear the term "mainstream" being thrown around. It is a term used to assert control on the part of the educrats.

Anti-Intellectual Progressive Education

Getting back to the *Cardinal Principles* of 1918, we can say two things about the document. It was apparently proposed to meet the needs of the new immigrants from Southern and Eastern Europe, whose language was not English. Before the recommendations of the *Principles* were put into effect, schools taught academic subjects such as history, languages (particularly Latin), mathematics, science and literature. The "Progressive" educators who proposed the *Principles* recommended areas such as "health, vocation, family membership, ethical character and the worthy use of leisure" (Hirsch, 48). At the same time, the *Principles* were antipathetic to academic subject matter. This point of view influenced and "dominated the training and certification of teachers in our teacher-training schools since the 1930s, that is, during the entire working lives of all persons teaching in our schools" (Hirsch, 49).

This hostility toward academic subject matter was exactly the opposite view of Antonio Gramsci. Although he was a Communist, he was not in tune with the progressive movement in education which was dedicated to introducing what is called "natural" and "practical." Gramsci, to reiterate, believed that the "practical" kind of education would keep the children of the poor in their place, ignorant and frozen in their economic and social condition.

We need only cite two guru educators quoted by Hirsch to indicate the hostility to academic subject matter. The first is William Heard Kilpatrick, an educator even more evangelical than John Dewey in pushing the cause of enlightened "progressive" education. In his *Foundations of Method* (1925) Kilpatrick says:

> *We are properly concerned first with children that they shall grow, and only secondarily with subject matter that it be learned…. Subject matter is good only and because it furnishes a better way-of-behaving…. The separate school subjects.[Sic] Shall we not have to give them up if the ideas of purposeful activity and intrinsic [Sic] subject-matter be adopted? As hitherto conceived and taught, yes; separate subjects for children would have to go (Hirsch, 109).*

Charles Prosser, another guru of "progressive" education says clearly and distinctly what he would deprive students from learning ---a learning, however, of which he himself was not deprived:

> *[B]usiness arithmetic is superior to plane or solid geometry; learning ways of keeping physically fit to the study of French; learning the technique of selecting an occupation, to the study of algebra; simple science of everyday life, to geology; simple business English to Elizabethan classics (Secondary Education and Life, Cambridge: Harvard U. Press, 1939, pp 15-16).*

In their wisdom to preach the practical, these gurus failed to learn the fallacy of the false alternative (or false disjunction). They also failed to learn what studies make people human. They should have paid more attention to their logic books. Then they would not have favored doing over knowing, the farmhouse over the school house, business arithmetic over plane geometry, the hammer over the book, the real world over the school (as if the school were not part of the real world). Although the gurus received a liberal education, they did not learn the lessons well. Nor have our more recent curriculum reformers who have no basis for preferring the study of Betty Friedan, Cornell West, or the Simpsons over Plato, Dante, or Shakespeare. Among other things, a sound liberal education would have done that for them. In the immortal words of Joseph Carpino, colleague, friend, and occupant of the stoop, "liberal education is the process of the student's self-'dejackassification.'" And later in the chapter we will say more about a "sound" liberal education. An argument can be made about the quality of students in any calculus of education, but this is not our argument. We leave this issue to others.

College — Where Minds Go To Die

The assorted "experts" who have mismanaged education for over a century learned the bad ideas while attending colleges and universities. Although the colleges and universities may still carry out teaching and learning, they are the laboratories of the bad ideas. What good they do are isolated mutations in their postmodern evolution.

Colleges and universities no longer promote a coherent academic program for undergraduate students. Surrendering to the pressures of cultural, moral, and epistemological relativism, subjectivism, and political correctness, colleges and universities invented "courses" to promote women's studies, black studies, gay studies — you name it, they got it. Colleges and universities abandoned their commitment to liberal academic education. Contemporary higher education is little more than an intellectual garage sale where amidst the junk you sometimes find a treasure; some valued reminder of Western Civilization.

As a consequence of abandoning their commitment to the traditional core curriculum in the arts and sciences, the organization and administration of colleges and universities have mutated accordingly for the worst. For example, the "emphasis on research" instead of teaching on the road to tenure compromises teaching and learning. The urge to "change the world," to do social work and psychological therapy has indeed changed the colleges and universities. In diverting their intellectual mission, they puffed up administrative bureaucracies purportedly needed to channel that urge. The abuse of the idea of adjunct faculty from assisting to replacing full time faculty erodes dedication to the profession. The mail-order and for-profit colleges and universities merit little comment except to say that they are pure products of the street hustler mentality in both the producer and consumer through the dialectic of deceiver and deceived. Do we need studies to prove this? Regrettably and disgracefully, colleges and universities are institutions of higher miseducation. As such they are repositories of propaganda, re-education, and indoctrination. They are places where minds, if they are not careful, go to die.

The Usual Suspects

This madness in education and elsewhere in the culture, as in science and art, does have a history and a hierarchical structure. It has its prophets and its priests, and those prophets and priests have their acolytes. They had the bad ideas and the charisma to execute them. Since anything that is bad presents itself in the guise of something good, as greed in regards to wealth or falsity in regard to truth, as lust in regard to love and as pornography in regard to sex, then we can understand how bad ideas catch on and develop. That is the big trick in the bag of tricks used by the prophets and priests of bad ideas. Remember, Satan was an angel, a creature of pure intelligence.

Such prophets and priests are armed with the resolute conviction of their cause and the self-righteous indignation which feeds it. As prophets and priests, they answer to no one, not even to God. That would require humility and modesty, qualities which their conviction and indignation could not abide. What we say here hangs together when we remember that the original sin in the Biblical account was one of disobedience to God's command not to eat of the fruit of the tree of knowledge of good and evil. Although presented in sexual imagery, the sin consisted in the usurpation of God's authority and in the scorn of human finitude and mortality. It consisted again in wanting to be not like God, but to be God, with full authority over life and death, over truth and falsity, over good and evil. Hence the idolatry and false prophets mentioned in the Bible, as man looked to hide from the face of God.

The biblical account, which exceeds the Promethean myth of man's punishment for the desire to know, is analogous to the views of the Sophists of ancient Greece, such as Protagoras, for whom Man is the measure of *all* things as he wades in the rivers of ever changing reality which Heraclitus recognized as the only reality (you should excuse the self-contradiction). Since change is reality and reality change, there is nothing that is permanently true or permanently false, nothing that is permanently good or permanently evil. As far as what to do is concerned for the individual sap, he must be content with mere opinion and not knowledge, with intense pleasure without pain and no virtue of any kind. Gorgias, another sophist of the same place and time, put the final touch to this oh, so sophisticated doctrine by asserting that nothing exists, only illusions; nothing is known, only perceived; nothing to say to another since there's nothing to say, and there is no other. Nihilism and solipsism come thus together in an impossible marriage. Nevertheless, the Sophists have successful prophets in many lands.

The Middle Ages in the West produced its own version of bad ideas that begat the madness of our times. There is a doctrine called nominalism which claims that only individuals exist. Universals do not exist. The individuals Oprah and Dr. Phil exist. Humanity does not exist in fact; only in word, in name. Truth and falsity, good and evil, beauty and ugliness do not exist objectively. They are only names that people decide to call groups of individual things, actions, or events. "Truth" is whatever we say is true; good is whatever we like or want; beauty is in the eye of the beholder; a family is just what a group of people decides to call itself. Talk about the primacy of the individual! Although St. Francis stuck his foot into this doctrine by insisting on the primacy of love over knowledge, one of his disciples, William of Ockham, the foremost exponent of nominalism and voluntarism in the 14th century, put it to words and the Beatles, in our time, put it to music when they crooned, "All you need is love."

When we enter the modern western world, a.k.a. Modernity, we encounter two prophets, Rousseau and the Marquis de Sade, in whom theory and practice meet to become an unholy mess of wanting to do anything and to experience everything. Against all that is evident to any observant and intelligent person, one of them proclaims that human beings are *naturally* good. Political life which Aristotle calls natural in order that human beings can become fully human in terms of art, science, and morality, i.e. the goal or *telos* of human life, Rousseau calls unnatural. "Man was born free and everywhere he is in chains." Here comes "the catcher in the rye!" Here comes "blue lagoon" educational theory. Here comes the guy who abused his women, disowned his own children, put them in orphanages and wrote for others his treatise on the education of children — *Emile* (1762). The use of the word "natural" in the lingo of progressivists in education comes from Rousseau through people like John Dewey. But the secret prophet, the secret king, the secret priest, the alpha and omega of the French Enlightenment, the one in whom madness is divine, the one for whom Cole Porter could have dedicated his song "Anything Goes," the man Rousseau would have liked to imitate as the perfect embodiment of the "natural" man — is the Marquis de Sade. And if, dear reader, you believe that we speak only of sexuality, you haven't understood a word of what we have said in the last few paragraphs.

The sin of Adam is to claim, like God, an infinite and unfettered will. The sin includes epistemological and moral relativism of the Sophists. It includes the nominalism and voluntarism of Ockham. It is the parody of the imitation of Christ in the imitation of Satan who chooses to rule in hell rather than serve in heaven. All are captured in the person of the Marquis de Sade — the cockeyed ikon, conscious or not, of such grandiose products of modernity as Josef Stalin, Adolph Hitler, and Mao Tse Tung.

The Acolytes

Brooklynite Diane Ravitch tells us in "Recycling Reforms" (*Education Next, 2004, No.1*) that education in America tends to be like religion, with cycles of stability and change, periodic crusades, and occasional bouts of zealotry and apostasy. The prophets of nihilism, relativism, determinism, and solipsism had done their jobs. It was the task of their acolytes to husband the Enlightenment project into our time. The history of modern education is littered with false premises masquerading as "theories" of education. According to those premises students have been described metaphorically as *lumps of plastic dough, blank tablets, machines, garden vegetables,* and *repositories of behaviors.* Each description led to its own school of education as the acolytes formed congregations and marched through modernity's seminaries, i.e., the halls of academia. Intellectual development and character development were abandoned while so called "practical reform movements" were imposed upon gullible congregations.

Herbert Spencer's whimsical belief that "progress" was a "beneficent necessity" influenced the writings of William James, Edward L. Thorndike, John Dewey, and G. Stanley Hall — the acolytes of the progressive movement. These "progressive" theorists insisted that education must attend to *children's nature,* their *modes of learning,* and their *stages of development.* These pronouncements about children explain how psychological, sociological, and anthropological theories supplanted traditional education as the formation of character, intelligence, and taste as the goals of education. What we mean by the traditional curriculum is that it was and is a liberal arts curriculum. It went by the Latin names of *Trivium* (Grammar, Logic, and Rhetoric) and *Quadrivium* (Arithmetic, Geometry, Music, and Astronomy). It aimed at freeing men and women from ignorance, bad habits, and bad taste. Spencer's dogmatic insistence on child-centered education stressing the importance of the child's experience disrupts the dialectic of the teacher-student relationship in shifting the emphasis away from the traditional content of the curriculum and the authority of the teacher to the *presumed* needs of the child.

The influence of Spencer, Dewey, and Piaget explains how the "stages of development" practices came to be used in schools today. Critics argued then and continue to argue now that this approach deprives children of challenging curricula and instruction and is based on unsubstantiated claims about "appropriate stages of development." Spencer and Dewey were Darwinian evolutionists and thus had to begin with simple empirical elements and work toward more complex elements. In their view, the child could not be understood as irreducibly complex in possessing both reason and will. Fundamentally, the error of Spencer, Dewey, Piaget, and the progressives is philosophical. They all significantly advanced the cause of maleducation at a time when it could have been arrested.

William James, G. Stanley Hall, and William Heard Kilpatrick represent the effort to replace traditional education with modern psychological "theories." The "child-centered" approach in curriculum was supposed to be implemented through "hands-on" learning, "portfolios" and "projects." Students were supposed to learn only what they need to know or can discover by themselves. It doesn't take a "college boy" to realize that the initial differences between children entering school would be exacerbated throughout their years of schooling. Weaker students are not challenged; as a result, they come out no better than when they started.

Reform in education, like the landscape of Brooklyn, is populated with many churches. The church of educational psychologists insisted that scientific testing methods would identify what should be studied and who should study it. After World War I, progressive modern education was "vocational" and "industrial" education. Junior high schools appeared and students were encouraged to make vocational decisions as early as age 12 or 13. Edward L. Thorndike led the way to the promised land of IQ testing. Educators could use IQ tests to discover a child's "natural ability" and "innate capacity." Educators could now direct children into the right program track.

One more example illustrates the extent, zeal, and fanaticism that are the madness in education. It has to do with the psychological theory of behaviorism which has and continues to have a great influence in education. B.F. Skinner was a famous American behaviorist. The behaviorists insist that children learn only through experience; thus, behaviorists generate the appropriate "stimulus" to produce the desired "response." Since rats and pigeons appear to learn this way, and since human beings are simply and merely different animals, then children should be taught in the same way. Skinner was so committed to behaviorism that he reared his infant daughter in a "Skinner box," a closed container with a window, outfitted with signaling levers and a food chute." Now that's commitment! John Taylor Gatto notes in his book, *The Underground History of American Education:* "Italian parents giving their own children a glass of wine in those days might have ended up in jail and their children in foster care, but what Skinner did was perfectly legal" (Gatto, 259).

Let us mention three other great American geniuses who had served as acolytes of modern education. John Dewey we have touched upon before. Can we trust apologists for Stalin and the Soviet Union when there were already many perceptive critics of that tyrant and his murderous regime? If so, then we can trust John Dewey whose political bad ideas matched in ignorance and stupidity those in education. For example, Dewey, after visiting schools in the Soviet Union, wrote in 1928 a series of articles in *The New Republic* where he stated: "I have never seen anywhere in the world such a large proportion of intelligent, happy, and intelligently occupied children." His much too late exercise in disappointment over Stalin and his socialist gulag does not purchase an indulgence for his bad ideas. It is regrettable that Brooklyn Existentialists must live with the fact that a public high school founded on his bad ideas and named after him is located in Brooklyn.

What are we to say about James Heard Kilpatrick, Columbia Teacher's College professor, who promoted the bad idea of "child-centered" education through "projects" which would not have been bad if it had not dismissed the importance of subject matter. It is no accident that Kilpatrick was flattered to learn that his writings on education had been translated into Russian and used to train Russian teachers. Current American orthodoxy in education does not mention how soon the Soviets abandoned Kilpatrick's bad ideas. Why? These bad ideas did not work. What the Soviets discovered from experience after a few years, American orthodoxy in education has yet to discover.

Remembering singer, Peggy Lee, we ask: "Is that all there is?" Our answer is, "No!" Not to single out Columbia, a former president of Harvard, James Conant, defined education as, "what goes on in schools." Conant has closed the circle. Shall we dance?

Liberal Education: Knowing What to Resist

What is supposed to go on in schools at the level of college and university is the completion of liberal education. The worries, the studies, the taxes, and the activities employed to reform education at each level are vain unless and until we recapture the purpose and content of liberal education. Modernity's success in health and welfare has not been met with a similar success in education. Given what's gone on, how could it. The twentieth century froths with enacted proposals and justifications for reform with such ideas as "progressive" education, charter schools, affirmative action, vouchers, "headstart," higher standards, sex education and much more. Just name the idea, and its acolytes rush in to support it with their hubris up and their hands out, notwithstanding the inverse proportion of taxes spent to results achieved. But if we are serious about recapturing the purpose and content of liberal education, a good start would be to subordinate process to substance so as to arrest the futility. This is the revolution, pardon the rhetoric, that must occur. It must go on modestly with a few distinctions that ignore the silly and mawkish exhortations about education for the twenty-first century or for the millennium. Additionally, it must avoid the now rebarbative appeals to "innovative" and "creative" theories of education — as if 2,500 years of history taught us nothing, or that current and future technology could transmogrify into substance.

Motives and Ends

The first distinction signifies the real difference between the motives for going to college or university on one hand and the primary goal of colleges and universities on the other. In most cases the motives, those of the students and their families, can be formulated as the attempt to improve their economic and social conditions through the avenue of higher education. This attempt is both understandable and even laudable as the reason for going to college and university. It is not, however, the primary goal of these institutions. Nevertheless, it *is* consistent with their secondary goals, which are to provide students with those skills and techniques required in the world of work. But that world of work, whether it be commerce or government, cannot and should not command or determine the primary goal of liberal education. Nor should those who form opinion in society always be trusted to designate the primary goal of liberal education. This includes those intellectuals who consider themselves *progressive* and occupy college and university faculties. Indeed, they are now even in charge of them. Such intellectuals conceive of liberal education as redemption from poverty and suffering and, admittedly at times, even ignorance.

They conceive of colleges and universities as instruments of social transformation or psychological therapy. As such these intellectuals appear righteous, but their influence has turned those institutions into degenerative instruments of their own primary goals. Colleges and universities are neither hospitals nor social clinics; nor are they churches of either the religious or secular kind. The transformation that coincides with the primary end of institutions of higher learning is the cultivation of the students' *minds* primarily, then derivatively their hearts and their actions in such a manner as befits liberally educated persons. It is with this end that colleges and universities prepare their students, not merely as business managers, lawyers, priests, physicians, accountants or teachers, but as human beings precisely in their humanity.

The Nature and End of Liberal Education

Liberal education, which lies at the center of every institution of higher education worthy of the name, commits that institution to excellence. As such, liberal education is that systematic cultivation of those qualities that make human beings excellent: reason and the freedom grounded in that reason. Those who believe otherwise, as Pascal once did when he said "the heart has its reasons which reason does not know," will have to bear with him the burden of that weighty paradox.

Liberal education begins with one's family and one's ethnic tradition, without forgetting them, as a snob would do, and moves toward the human heritage. In this transition the student moves back and forth from *societas* to *civilitas*, from society to civilization. The important aspect and specific difference of college or university education is that it builds upon, and then moves beyond primary and secondary education. At the first two levels, students are formed and informed about their own culture in a process begun in the family. They are, on those levels, to be trained in those basic and necessary skills in reason, language, and computation through which they will act as workers and citizens and by which they are prepared to learn the more specialized skills of their professions.

The college education continues this liberation from ignorance on one hand and also from an *unconscious* dependence upon authority and traditions on the other. It is both *educare*, to rear and to bring up, and *educere*, to lead out and go forth. The movement from ethnic to human heritage is analogous to the movement of learning, which begins in perceptions and opinions and moves toward truth and knowledge. While the quest for knowledge does not forget its origin in perceptions and opinions, so too the quest for the human as such does not forget its beginnings in ethnicity, race, sex, or class. For human beings are not angels; nor are they Gnostic caricatures. They are not minds trapped in bodies; nor are they mindless bodies. But they are, miraculously, human; this means that they cannot and must not be restricted to the particularities of ethnicity, race, sex, or class.

Liberal education is not, therefore, a reflection, a repetition, or an echo of fashionable opinions and actions, of media psychology and sociology — a gaggle of clichés, platitudes, and acronyms which vitiate learning, deaden moral sensibility, and extinguish freedom. Rather liberal education consists in the formation of the whole person in a proper harmony of intelligence, character, and taste — a harmony often fatuously expressed in the cliché "well-rounded." Liberal education does not consist in the production of dilettantes who believe and would have others believe that their education has prepared them for highfalutin' talk about all manner of things, weighty or otherwise. Liberal education is not a process wherein the Socratic "finding out for oneself" or the development of one's intelligence, character, and taste is a rejection of tradition and authority as such, only of the blind and unconscious slavery to them. Such "finding out for oneself" is an exercise in the discernment of what should be accepted and what should be scorned in the pursuit of truth, goodness, and beauty — the ends or goals for which intelligence, character, and taste exist and are exercised.

The education that is liberal is just as resistant to producing hedonists without character as it is to producing technicians without imagination, if we may take liberties with Max Weber's insight. Indeed it is a preparation, in the practical order, above all else, for the terrors of life, so that when failure or even tragedy occurs, the liberally educated person can face it and not be destroyed by it. And if such tragedy as the debasement of civilization occurs, we must hope that some such persons will be found to re-establish it.

If, then, liberal education tries to develop free and rational men and women who are concerned with the pursuit of knowledge, and who are conscious of their moral and social duties, or to put it another way, if liberal education is the formation of persons capable of responsible self-determination, for it is in this that freedom consists, then the test for them will be not only what they recognize as worthy of *pursuit* but also what they deem necessary to *resist*. The seven deadly sins, for instance — pride, envy, greed, lust, sloth, wrath, and gluttony — present themselves today through the cunning charms of what Robert Bork called "high tech barbarism," to which we add its companion — cheap sentimentality (as in such effusions as "I feel your pain" or "We are the world").

The pursuit of knowledge, not to speak of the pursuit of power, of wealth, of pleasure, and of fame, on the part of liberally educated persons should always be subject to the moderating rule of reason, which Aristotle called "*phronesis*." Then the extremes of excess and defect would be avoided. Freedom will consist in liberal mastery over one's opinions and over one's passions, whether they be of the erotic or aggressive sort. Mastery over opinions will consist in the straightforward ability to explain and justify them. We speak here of freedom of thought, not freedom of expression. Dominion over passions will disclose itself in an ennobling expression of them, both to oneself and to others. It is then that students will be best suited to learn and master the special skills of their professions, and to become competent, responsible and mature citizens and not the moral rebels so consciously cultivated and celebrated in the imperial and manipulative media as transgressive.

In their relationships with others, persons who are liberally educated will give and accept service graciously. They will pursue learning together, enjoying the company of like-minded, independent, and confident people. They will avoid or keep under control those people who know only two postures: to be at someone's feet or at someone's throat. They will surely avoid those postures themselves. Rather, they will render respect and friendship, not flattery or hostility. They will have "learned to respect," as Eva Brann said in a commencement address at St. John's College Annapolis in 1974, "ordinary plodding decent humanity which [they] must acknowledge not only in [themselves] but cherish in others." This ordinariness, Brann continued, "is not the opposite of excellence but is the ground from which excellence grows." The true opposites of this ordinariness are barbarism and intellectualism. The first is the embodiment of mindless passion; the other is the abstraction of passionless mind. Liberal education aims at resisting both these monstrosities.

The Core Curriculum

The fundamental instrument of such liberal education has been forged in several ways. In the middle ages it was called the liberal arts, i.e., the *trivium* (logic, grammar, and rhetoric) and the *quadrivium* (arithmetic, geometry, music, and astronomy). As such, it combined the study of the humanities and the sciences. Today it is done through a core curriculum, or through a study of great books which is not so closed a "canon" as its critics would have us believe. Or it might be done in some other ways, as through topics. A core curriculum would ordinarily incorporate many of the great books (East and West, North and South). But the concept and fact of a core curriculum has been under attack for the last half of the twentieth century, while the concept and fact of the great books has been under attack for a long time.

The core is that part of a college or university's curriculum in the arts and sciences that is *required* of all students and provides for a systematic cultivation of the qualities discussed earlier. Those who cringe at the notion of requirements fail or do not wish to recognize the different responsibilities of teachers and students. Determining curriculum is a responsibility of a "responsible" faculty, not of students; else they would not be students. Studying and learning the curriculum is the responsibility of students.

The core is distinct from the major program and also from the elective courses precisely in its aim of preparing students for the rest of their lives by uniting their professions with the values of their common human heritage. This aim consists in their speaking, reading, and writing effectively through the study of the national language and the communication arts (what used to be called rhetoric); in understanding their own culture and the culture of others through the study of languages, the fine arts, religion and the social or behavioral sciences; in investigating the order and structure of nature and to learn the scientific method through the study of the physical sciences; in understanding the human past for itself, as an instruction for the present, and as a guide for the future by means of the study of history; in developing analytic and synthetic habits of mind through the study of mathematics and philosophy; in probing the issue of value and values through the study of religion, the social sciences, and philosophy; in distinguishing the basic conceptual alternatives as well as the foundations and implications of the various types of discourse through the study of philosophy; and in cultivating the life of the mind through the ideal of scholarship as a distinct value by means of all the disciplines in the core curriculum.

The conception of liberal education defined, described, and explained above is not the only conception, as Richard Burke pointed out in a splendid but ignored essay entitled "Two Concepts of Liberal Education" and published in *Academe*, the journal of the American Association of University Professors, the October 1980 issue. It is a Platonic conception in that it is systematic, hierarchical, and teleological. It can be called scientific in that it seeks to know first principles. Certain things must be studied, i.e., there is a prescribed curriculum in an order from simple to more complex or advanced. As such it is also dialectical. The things to be studied are directed toward ends such as those mentioned above: intelligence, character, and taste, which in turn are directed toward truth, goodness, and beauty. Plato's conception, which can be found in the *Republic*, maintains that freedom, as we said before, is grounded on reason, i.e., decisions or choices are free insofar as they are deliberative. This occurs through thought, discovering certain standards of objectivity or truth, otherwise the ideas and choices are arbitrary.

Liberal Education and General Education

Consequently, the second distinction is between liberal education and general education, a distinction Burke had made but which has been forgotten. Liberal education is not general education. In the program of general education, all courses are of equivalent value. They are arranged in area concentrations, often mockingly referred to as the "Chinese menu" curriculum. They are often the result of political compromise between faculty members or departments, or current fashions in education. Liberal education refers to the goals of the process; general education refers to the collection or range of the material studied, as selected by individual students. The students put the curriculum together themselves, perhaps — and that is a big "perhaps" — with the guidance of advisors. Its aim is to acquaint students with some areas of human theory and practice.

A Counterfeit Version of Liberal Education

Our final distinction, also made by Burke, is concerned with still another conception of liberal education that is in contrast to the one propounded herein. It is one that draws inspiration from Protagoras, a philosophical adversary to Plato. This conception is succinctly expressed in the middle of Plato's dialogue, *Theaetetus*. It can be called "rhetorical," not in the superficial journalistic sense, but in the sense of students primarily being able to participate in a conversation about principles, rather than in the pursuit and attainment of first principles. It may be systematic and hierarchical but the system is utilitarian and the hierarchy is one of temporal succession, insofar as some subjects are to be studied before others. There is no commitment to subject matters being studied for their own sake or for transcendent ends. A liberally educated person in this sense can carry on an intelligent discussion on any issue whatsoever, having been exposed to a multiplicity of subject matters. In this conception of liberal education, it is not important for students to be committed to any particular ideas or to read certain certified authors (as in the Great Books program). They should learn to present themselves effectively, whatever their ideas may be, and how to recognize the principles and methods of others. They should be exposed to as many different views and assumptions as possible. Process takes precedence over contents. Eastern thought as well as Western should be studied without regarding either as superior, only different. Ancient and modern societies are to be studied without odious comparisons. In the study of language, any language will do. Classical languages have no privilege or priority. In the study of literature, *I, Rigoberta Menchú* shares honors with *King Lear.* Astrology is as worthy of study as astronomy. The goal, if it can be called such, is to expose students to the variety of human perspectives, and cultivate tolerance for all of them. None is to be spurned or rejected. To do otherwise is to be dogmatic — the tyranny of one point of view over others when there are *only* points of view. The voices from the stoop warn the students to beware of this seductive invitation to liberal education for it would captivate them with the scent of a rosy world of sharing opinions and cultures. On the contrary, it is a world of shadows and imitation where substance does not exist. It is a world where falsity, evil and ugliness do not really exist. In extolling the differences of opinions and cultures that one welcomes and those that one rejects.

In the students' quest for knowledge--excuse us--opinions, they find a tawdry facsimile where the shadows are long and the substance is short.

CHAPTER TWO:
Dysfunctional Behavioral Sciences

To find out what "goes on in schools," you need to look at the "disciplines" that have done the most damage to common sense realism in forming the opinions of people about ordinary life – opinions that have loomed large in the madness of the 20th century and onward. Those disciplines have been blessed with the name of the social or behavioral sciences. To be specific, we speak of psychology, sociology, and sociology's child, anthropology. Since economists themselves call their "science" the "dismal science," we will take them at their word and say little or nothing about economics or economic theories. Besides, economic science has not done the intellectual and moral damage that the others have.

Not to be stupid about the matter, we acknowledge that our criticisms allow for exceptions and degrees. The social sciences have made contributions to the understanding about the particulars of the human condition and thus there is a place for them in the domain of human knowledge. Regrettably, some social scientists don't know that place. They have wandered into and trespassed on the territories of ideology, epistemology, and metaphysics. Those in the physical sciences and mathematics have doubts about whether the social sciences are indeed sciences at all, despite the fact that their studies are adorned with mathematical artifacts such as graphs, charts, and tables.

In the late 19th and early 20th centuries, what came to be called psychology, sociology, and anthropology were torn away from their philosophical moorings by their guru mandarins to modernity's cheers of liberation. The euphoria is duly recorded in the standard textbooks. These "sciences" have continued to drift ever since, swept along by the winds and carried on the tides of irrationalism, relativism, and finally nihilism. To paraphrase the theme-song of the mawkish movie *Love Story:* Where do we begin? We begin with some anecdotes.

Return with us now to those thrilling days of yesteryear when we sat in high school or college classrooms and were told that we were lost and had to find ourselves. Had we had Brooklyn Existentialists as our teachers, we might have been asked: What do you mean you're lost? You are in Brooklyn. You are on Remsen Street. You are in Saint Francis College. You took the subway to get here. You'll get home the same way. You're not lost. You've confused geographical location with psychological nonsense. Here's the cure for your confusion. Grasp your head firmly with both hands and pull it out of your backside. Once free, insert it into a book and study. To quote the rock band, *Yes,* "Don't surround yourself with yourself." And don't think that the greatest love there is — is the love of self — no matter how much you liked Whitney Houston's rendition of the song.

When will you be lost? It's when you try to live according to such slogans as: think outside the box; follow your bliss; go with the flow; and if it feels good — do it. This is the advice of the guru mandarin twits who are found in the fields of psychology and sociology. They did not merely lose their way, they lost the map. Yet this is the kind of "cutting edge" advice, propaganda, and indoctrination we get by way of the classroom and the media. The problem is that when most people think outside the box, they do in fact get lost. The mandarin twits have failed us again. Their advice ignores and dismisses the structure, integrity, and purpose of the box. No offense but, we say again "a man has got to know his limitations."

In addition to being "lost," we complain about being stressed and depressed. To relieve that stress and depression, we are urged by therapists and counselors to get in touch with our feelings, find our inner-child, find who we really are, and tell someone, preferably a therapist, about our feelings. Does this work? Of course not! The cure is much simpler. When you are feeling depressed – Skip! You can skip to work, you can skip to class. We have never seen anyone skipping who is not smiling. We have seen people leaving the therapist's office often sad and sometimes crying. Fitness gurus instruct us about the beneficial effects of raising endorphin levels by running. Can we expect less from skipping?

These anecdotes illustrate but do not explain the nonsense embedded in the ideas and practices preached by the guru mandarins of the "sciences" of psychology, sociology, and anthropology. Acknowledging exceptions and degrees, let us consider the origins of the "science" of psychology. The preoccupation with "adjusting" the human machine" emerged from the laboratory of Wilhelm Wundt at the University of Leipzig. Wundt constructed into a "science" the psychological manipulation of persons. His gospel was spread by such enthusiastic disciples of this science as G. Stanley Hall, Ivan Pavlov, John B. Watson and Edward L. Thorndike. It was G. Stanley Hall who invited Dr. Sigmund Freud to give a series of lectures in America at the turn of the 20th Century. The therapeutic society and the psychologized classroom, achieved through behaviorism and psychoanalysis, are the result of the "cutting edge" work of Wundt. Manipulation replaced education. Armed with an assortment of intelligence and psychological tests, "social scientists" and even eugenicists, we might add, could prove statistically anything and everything. Common sense realism nearly drowned in a tsunami of scientistic bad ideas. In the name of describing and explaining the human condition, these guys got into and played around with people's heads. To illustrate the point, college boy Johnny, after one psychology course, comes home and asks his mother about her sex life, his father about his fascination with tools, his sister about her penis envy, and his brother about his sibling rivalry.

The Dysfunction in Psychology

The greater and higher madness is not the existence and number of crazy people in the world. It is the objective madness of the so called science of psychology itself. Unlike those gurus playing at psychology like R.D. Laing who denies the existence of lunatics and calls their lunacy a way of coping with a crazy world, common sense says that there *are* crazy people. Unlike those other gurus who say that everyone is crazy and needs therapy, common sense says that most people are *not* crazy. There are events in the lives of ordinary people that make them happy (a better term than "euphoric") and other events that make them melancholy (a better term than "depressed").

In order to illustrate what we mean by "the objective madness of psychology" itself, one has but to look at some of the language used in psychology to demonstrate how it corrupts language and distorts events and things. It happens by way of euphemisms, falsehoods, and lies. The post-modernists, who follow Nietzsche and say that all language is metaphorical — that there are no literal truths — are correct if they limit that assertion to much of the language of psychology and sociology. Hence the allusions to psycho-babble and socio-babble on the part of critical common sense realists. It does not inspire confidence in the claims that psychology is scientific when such psychology professors as Philip Zimbardo are reported as saying (*Newsweek*, 4/11/75) that madness is "subjective." He must have been kidding. Is this the Zimbardian version of "it's all in the mind," a double irony if there ever was one. Madness is in the mind, i.e., madness is about the mind and therefore subjective but there is no real madness only subjective definitions of it. This is the sociopaths "get out of jail card." What about Elizabeth Kubler-Ross, the founder of the "death and dying movement" talking about facing death on one hand, then denying that death exists on the other (*New York Times Magazine*, 1/22/95)?

If there is any sophist out there thinking that this stuff is just anecdotal, he should think about actions on the part of the psychiatric profession when it succumbed to political correctness and in 1974 removed homosexuality from the list of mental disorders in its handbook (*The Diagnostic and Statistical Manual of the American Psychiatric Association, II Edition*). We are not saying that homosexuality belonged on the list of mental disorders, but the psychiatrists did; and then they changed their minds. Can we expect them to change their minds again? Then in the third edition of 1980, the *DSM* announced that a homosexual believing his homosexuality to be a mental disorder is now a mental disorder. The *DSM* implies that every part of human life (except psychiatry) can be interpreted as crazy. There you are: It's official: everyone is crazy and, of course, everyone needs therapy.

This is not all there is. Take account of the epistemology of psychology characterized by Robert J. Samuelson in *Newsweek* (5/9/94), as "[t]he triumph of the psycho-fact." This is to say that if we *feel* a statement is true, then it is, even if it isn't. *Perception* of things, persons, and events trumps and supersedes the *reality* of things, persons, and events. What are ordinary citizens and even college boys to say about the scientific credibility of psychology and psychiatry as they are used in courts of law when insanity pleas are made? People do wonder about how scientific those fields can be if expert witnesses testify on opposite sides of an insanity plea in a criminal case. Is insanity a description of behavior or an interpretation? Where's the science? This stuff is beyond parody. But don't laugh yet. In fact you won't be able to laugh at all when you think about the words spawned by these "sciences" and its success in distorting minds. Regrettably, the behavioral sciences have controlled the public discourse.

Here is a list of terms in current usage. Most of the terms begin in the field of academic psychology or sociology, are then applied in therapeutic practice, and from there trickle down to the pop-psych discourse of laymen. There are words and phrases whose presence on this list of bad ideas will annoy those who thought them to be "scientific" and still other words will annoy those who have a vested interest in their use: "anal fixation, oral fixation, role playig, role model, sensitivity training, judgmental, profiling, reverse role playing, grief counselors, inclusive, diversity, id, superego, oppositional defiant disorder, obsessive compulsive, paranoid schizophrenic, self-esteem, physically challenged, bi-polar, affirmative action, multiculturalism, relationship, attention deficit disorder, social anxiety disorder, teenager (as a category), sexworkers, undocumented workers, workshops, vulnerability, facilitator, undeveloped fetus, self-actualization, nothing is black or white, nontraditional patriotism."

Most of these terms can be expressed in literate ordinary language, as for example, talkative for oral type, a collector for anal type, meddlers for grief counselors, preferential treatment for affirmative action, illegal immigrants for undocumented workers, neat and tidy for obsessive compulsive, inattentive for attention deficit disorder, hate or fear of crowds for social anxiety disorder, conscience for superego, love affair or marriage for relationship, prostitutes or ladies of the bordello for sexworkers, hero for role model, and unborn child for undeveloped fetus.

Some of these corruptions have philosophical presuppositions such as role, role playing, and role reversal. The presupposition here is that people do not have identities; they play roles. Being wives, mothers, teachers are just roles not realities of people's lives. The realities may change over the course of a life but they are not roles on a stage despite Shakespeare's metaphor in *As You Like It*.

As therapy, role playing and sensitivity training are dangerous especially when used in issues of sex, race, and ethnicity. They amount to little more than politically correct manipulation and self-manipulation. We leave it to the reader to translate those terms we have left untranslated. The terms are used well and properly when they are mocked from stoops all over Brooklyn.

Lunacy Heights: From Insects to Incest

The Prince of Promiscuity, Alfred Kinsey, parlayed a *bona fide* career in entomology into a legacy as the Pied Piper of deviance. His preoccupation with variation drove him to collect millions of specimens of gall wasps. But his meteoric rise did not begin until he turned his attention to a very different WASP (a paradigm for an uptight human being). His notoriety is not based on his collection of insects but rather on his collection of sexual histories.

Kinsey, true to Darwinian dogmatism, transferred his curiosity about individual variation among gall wasps to an overreaching generalization about variability in the world of living things and, Q.E.D, said variability must be intrinsic in human sexual behavior; unless, of course, society intervenes. Who knew that human behavior was foreshadowed in the lives of bugs? Move over trousered apes and make room for the clothed gall wasp. Variation in gall wasps, driven by Darwinian evolution, legitimized Kinsey's obsession with pornography and deviance under the cover of the scientific study of "human sexuality." Deviant sexual behavior was merely a sign of "random beneficial mutations" in the inevitable progress of human society. The appearance of science was sufficient to persuade an eager public to transform and distort education, law, and morality.

Kinsey's "empirical" evidence came from the sexual histories of homosexuals, prostitutes, prison inmates and pedophiles. From this restricted sample, he made generalizations about the nature of human sexual behavior. He ignored the criticisms of contemporaries and insisted that his samples were not biased. Anyone who has even a cursory knowledge of elementary statistics knows that the validity of a study is compromised when the data are skewed or when conclusions are based on the responses of "volunteers." More recent challenges have targeted Kinsey's fixation on homosexual behavior. Kinsey's desire, however, to subvert morality and sexual norms resonated with the public. Kinsey's preoccupation with "boy-play" provided scientific credibility for Hugh Hefner's magazine, *Playboy*. Let the good times roll.

Kinsey and his "researchers" went beyond interviews and gave new meaning to the phrase "hands-on" science in their notorious child "experiments" to document the incidence of orgasm in pre-adolescents. His belief that human beings are pansexual shattered any sensible regard for modesty, decency, and innocence in the maturation of young children. Consequently, the view that adult sex with children is harmless has attracted increased support in the last 50 years. Wardell Pomeroy, the Dean of the Institute for the Advanced

Study of Human sexuality, promoted incest as beneficial when advising readers of *Penthouse*, *Chic* and other pornographic magazines.

Critics and common sense realists want to know who provided the repeated stimulation necessary for these "subjects," that is, children, to reach orgasm. Was it provided by pedophiles? In that case, it's worthless. Was it the result of Kinsey's researchers participating in the experiments? In that case, it was the result of criminal activity. And finally, where was the public and media outrage when the data were reported? Kinsey exploited a zoologist's taxonomy to give the appearance of science as he collected, organized, and classified child molestation. Lest we forget, this "hero" of sexual liberation and human progress was rewarded by the cultural elite for his efforts with a "major motion picture," *Kinsey* (2004), a film as devoid of science as his books.

The Dysfunction in Sociology

Although he was preceded by such positivist students of society as Claude Saint-Simon, it is August Comte who is the acknowledged "father" of sociology and of positivism. Positivism indeed is the doctrine that science alone yields facts, that is, knowledge about the world. Although earlier commentators wrote about human science, sociology after Comte claimed to study society "scientifically." By that accounting, religion consists of myth and poetry; philosophy, at best, only of the logical organization of facts. That is why some facts about sociology's father are interesting: namely, that he thought that sociologists would eventually become the *priests* of a new age; that he saw himself as the *pontifex maximus* of a new religion; that he published a *catechism* for this new positivist religion; that he was sexually obsessed with a younger woman, though frustrated by impotence; and that he was subject to occasional episodes of lunacy.

What we have here is a scientistic religion of humanity, the third stage in the law of evolutionary history replacing the theological (or "fictitious") first stage and the metaphysical (or abstract) second stage. Talk about, you should pardon the expression, "the return of the repressed!" With such an auspicious beginning, it is no wonder that the "sciences" of sociology and anthropology are joined with psychology in creating the sociobabble and psychobabble intended to control and manipulate the subjects, i.e., human beings, the ones that they are supposed to describe and explain. Rejecting the "archaic" and "useless" concepts of good and evil and of right and wrong, positivism anticipated the "scientific" cure for all human problems.

Is it any wonder that these "sciences" wish to hide behind the curtain of being "value free," that is, concerned only with facts, and thereby making no value judgments in their study of human beings in society? In the first place, the sophomoric claim to be value free — to be purely scientific — to be solely factual — is a value judgment of the very basic kind, opening that claim to the "intolerant" and "unenlightened" charge of self-contradiction. In the second place, wishing to treat all societies alike and equal is another level of value-judging. As the Wizard says, in *The Wizard of Oz*, "Pay no attention to the man behind the curtain."

As a reminder, we call attention to the rubric of differences and degrees so as to mention, without naming them, those honest sociologists, anthropologists and psychologists who are scientific without the dogma and who recognize the fact-value distinction and recognize as well the reciprocal relationship between them.

But these social scientists are not those who got control of the discourse and through that control got to distort human life as soft tyrants, but tyrants nevertheless, who dictate to their subject-slaves what and how to think and what and how to feel. It is the tyranny of what E. Michael Jones in his book, *Degenerate Moderns* (1993), calls "blue lagoon" anthropology (Jones, 43) and what Aldous Huxley called the brave new world in his novel of that same name. The schools and universities which were once the institutions of liberation through the pursuit of knowledge have now become the seminaries of politically correct servitude by means of tolerance, diversity, and sexual propaganda. Criticism of these politically correct doctrines is routinely suppressed. Challengers are marginalized and blacklisted. Academic freedom is mere rhetoric to distract an unsuspecting and trusting public. The possibility of truth and freedom are still alive in corners of the West, as in Brooklyn U.S.A., but as smoldering embers.

The Frankfurters

Among the most influential of the soft tyrants in the social sciences are members of "the Frankfurt School" in Germany. Mindful of Freud and Kinsey on the issue of sex, we find resonance in the Frankfurt Schooler, Wilhelm Reich, who wrote a book, *Die Sexualität in Kulturkampf* (1936; English edition *The Sexual Revolution, 1945*), which was more advocacy than description or explanation. To this alchemist, science owes the discovery of cosmic sexual energy called "Orgone." He believed, practiced and preached the religion of sex as the best instrument to use for social control and revolution against Western, especially Catholic, morality and political order. Feed their vices and control their lives. This is the deepest meaning of pornography. Of course, though morally wrong, he was correct. For what is as seductive as sex, except the lust for power, to turn people away from the moral law. This comes as no surprise to those who have read in the Bible about the struggle between the Babylonian fertility cults and Yahwistic religion. There is no guessing where Reich stood in that struggle. In his *Mass Psychology of Fascism* (1933) he recommends masturbation as liberation, the glorious mysteries of which can be found in the feminist liberation memoirs of such disciples as Lisa Palac, Elizabeth Wurtzel and Sara Tisdale. Masturbation in the hands of feminists becomes sacramental.

Reich's promotion of masturbation *vorhanden and zuhanden* (at hand and to hand) as Martin Heidegger would say, is a powerful and, dare we add, handy weapon for the culture war against Catholic morality. What better way is there to find and get a grip on oneself? His conjoining of Catholicism and fascism, a bit of magic he does with fellow Frankfurter, Theodor Adorno, who in *The Authoritarian Personality* (1950) "explains" fascism as arising from the sexual repression found in the Catholic Church which is the institutionalization of patriarchy, hierarchy, tradition, authoritarianism, anti-Semitism, and of course, sexual repression and fascism. In his sometime harmony with the Frankfurters, Hungarian philosopher and fellow Marxian, Georg Lukacs, asked literally and rhetorically: "Who will free us from Western Civilization?" And Erich Fromm, another Frankfurter, added to the litany of oppression — capitalism as the Calvinist Protestant contribution to Western Civilization which in the economic order enshrines inequality with authoritarianism. Here too he could have blamed Catholicism; for prior to the Protestant ethic, the instruments of capitalism, banking and accounting, already existed in Catholic Florence and Siena.

Still another Frankfurter, Herbert Marcuse, a guru of the '60s New Left, encouraged his disciples to become servile appendages of their sex organs by making "love not war." Then he thanked America for her hospitality, after fleeing from the Nazis, by calling her freedoms "repressive tolerance." So much for gratitude.

The Frankfurters with their Coney Island Dreamland and Luna Park fantasies should have gone to Nathan's in the real Coney Island (Brooklyn, U.S.A.) for a bite of reality; that is, of some authentic frankfurters. Eating franks by the sea would have provided the old geezer horny intellectuals with real food and good thoughts to kill the viruses in their brains. For those men and women who caught those viruses, what can we say? Franks at Nathan's; pizza and beer at Totonno's — Brooklyn Existentialism's antidote for bad ideas, inasmuch as good ideas never entered their minds. It is hard to imagine the Frankfurters ever having a dark night of the soul. Depression? Yes. Dark night? No.

Lest anyone "feel" that our treatment of the Frankfurt School, its disciples and friends, in the form of puns and street ridicule is overdone and unserious, the voices from the stoop insist that it is precisely this form of street ridicule that their ideas deserved but generally did not get. Although Socrates was not guilty of disbelieving in God (albeit disbelieving in the gods of Athens) and corrupting the youth, the members of the Frankfurt School were. Street ridicule is indeed the enlightened response to bad ideas. The words are *les mots juste*.

Paving the Way for the Age of Aquarius

In *The Long March* (2000), Roger Kimball writes that his aim is "to show how many of the ideals of the counterculture have quietly triumphed in the afterlife of the '60s and what that triumph has meant for America's cultural and intellectual life." He argues that prophets such as Nietzsche, Marx and Freud were "antecedents" to the origins of the cultural revolution of the 1960s. The immediate energy came from "the emergence of the Beats" — for example, the poet Allen Ginsberg and the novelists William S. Burroughs and Jack Kerouac. The path from the prophets to the Beats who preached drug use, free love, irrationalism, and strident anti-Americanism was clear. With Oz looming on the horizon, second-team mediaries such as Ruth Benedict, Margaret Mead, and Abraham Maslow paved the yellow brick road to utopia in the Age of Aquarius.

The fuss made over the '50s by the '60s generation as the decade of benighted thought and repressed lives betrayed a colossal and willful ignorance of history. The '50s were imagined as the foil for the enlightened and liberated '60s. The truth is that the images of the '50s in the minds of the *sessantini* (Italian for the '60s rebels) came from television, especially from such shows as "Leave it to Beaver," "Father Knows Best" and "Ozzie and Harriet." Although they were only shows, they were family shows about family life. The *sessantini*, or as the French put it more specifically, *les soixante huitards* (the sixty-eighters), saw the enemy, i.e., traditional family life and traditional morality, in their recollection of these shows. Coming from the American establishment of the time, these privileged darlings even had their own founding document, the Port Huron Statement (1962). This evangelical treatise from the new left showed how "idealistic" they were in their riots and romps, marked by a zealous indignation and patronizing condescension so characteristic of "idealists." The Free Speech Movement at the University of California, Berkeley (1964) complemented the founding document of the revolution. It defined its rhetorical posture as a declaration of freedom for profanity and vulgarity.

Those shows were, however, *their* shows, thereafter mocked and rejected. It was not incidental that the '60s rebels took their ideas of the historical '50s from the fictions of television. Appearance and image were replacing reality. The '50s were more their decade than those of their parents who made their mark in the '30s and '40s and who were labeled "the greatest generation" by such pundits as Tom Brokaw, telejournalist filter of information. It was members of this greatest generation, the combatants of the Great Depression and World War II, who were the parents of the '60s rebels and who were viewed as the oppressors. Remember the slogan: "Don't trust anyone over 30." What is more, it was in the '50s that the scouting parties for the revolution of the '60s appeared; namely, the lives and works of the Beat Generation, who used and touted recreational sex and drugs to achieve beat-if-cation. It was in the '50s as well that "Rock and Roll" became the liturgical music of the revolution to be, reaching its zenith in the Woodstock Concert of 1969 where the cultural revolution marched in the uniform of jeans to the tune of "sex, drugs, and rock and roll." It was in the '50s that hip-swiveling Rock Star, Elvis Presley, became the image of Rock Stars to come. It was in the '50s that the rebel (actor James Dean) and the outsider (author Colin Wilson), trading on the mystique of the American Revolution, became hero and icon. Simply put, the terms "rebel" and "outsider" became honorifics with transgression as the accepted parody of courage.

The Vietnam War began in the '50s and the protests against it in the '60s provided the occasion and cover for this deeper and longer-lasting cultural revolution. The just cause grievances of African Americans received a strong impetus from the controverted constitutionality of the Supreme Court decision, *Brown v. Board of Education of 1954*. Just cause grievances became the civil rights doctrine and laws of the '60s which in turn became the Marxist-Leninist Black Power movement with its attendant rhetoric and violence. '50s feminists such as Betty Friedan and Bella Abzug, with their Marxist doctrines about Capitalism and the traditional family structure as oppressors of women, gave birth to the radical feminism of the '60s Feminist liberation climaxing in the monumental but unconstitutional abortion rights Supreme Court decision of 1973. The feminist movement was accompanied by the American Indian movement and by the homosexual rights movement. Then the list of victims extended to animals, other than humans, to trees and finally to the global environment; all of which became institutionalized in school curricula together with policies of affirmative action for students, faculties, and administrators enforced by the power of the federal government. The Western interest in religions of the East was also part of the movement which had antecedents in the '50s; the enthusiasms of Alan Watts for Zen Buddhism; not to speak of Joseph Campbell's studies of myths as overdoses of religious relativism.

The point: events of the '50s such as calls for revolution and liberation led to the events of the '60s. The formative bad ideas came earlier, however, from the guru-mandarins treated elsewhere in our account and on whom the greater responsibility rests for the objective madness of our times. In the movie *Chinatown* (1974), a character, describing the horror and incomprehensibility of the concluding scene says: "Forget it, Jake. It's Chinatown!" To describe the lunacy of the guru mandarins, we add not only Chinatown but Xanadu.

The 1928 publication of *Coming of Age in Samoa* by Margaret Mead was a telling moment in the rise of cultural relativism. The introduction was written by Franz Boas and it was reviewed by Ruth Benedict. Joyce Milton, in her book, *Malpsychia,* says that Benedict "praised her lover's work in the pages of the *Journal of Philosophy* and the *New Republic*" (Milton, 29). With such an intellectual pedigree, it entered the canon of authoritative research in anthropology. "Every literate American could rest assured that 'science' had proven that teenage sexuality could be wholesome and beautiful, if only parents and 'society' would stop interfering" (Milton, 29). *Coming of Age in Samoa* was required reading in the social sciences for most of the 20th century. Anyone with doubts or criticisms of Mead's research methods dare not challenge the authority of Franz Boas and Ruth Benedict. Margaret Mead became the celebrity of cultural relativism.

Derek Freeman, however, did challenge Mead's overreaching generalizations in *Margaret Mead in Samoa* (1983) and again in *The Fateful Hoaxing of Margaret Mead* (1999). That challenge occurred long after the corrosive effects of Mead's spurious research had been achieved. Intellectuals enthusiastically embraced the ethos of sexual promiscuity based on a nine month study by a Columbia graduate student. In his trenchant summary of Freeman's refutation of Mead's research, E. Michael Jones writes: "Freeman claimed that Mead as the student of Boas had subordinated scientific considerations to the ideology of cultural relativism. She had tailored her data to suit the ideology she went there to substantiate" (Jones, 28). Mead used the appearance of science to advocate the prevailing world view of intellectuals. Mead's poetic description of Samoan adolescents provides little insight into human nature other than what one can expect when the search for truth is confused with advocating ideology. "*Coming of Age in Samoa* was in effect *Blue Lagoon anthropology*" (Jones, 33). Mead's lesbian relationship with Ruth Benedict, her extra-marital affairs, and her three husbands support the conclusion reached by E. Michael Jones in *Degenerate Moderns*: Mead's fictional account of Samoan adolescents is little more than "rationalized sexual misbehavior." Mead's research is an excuse for her violations of the moral law. Her success and popularity through most of the 20th century illustrate modernity's compromised intellectual standards.

The oversimplification that opposites attract is confirmed, however, in the love affair between the public and provocative Margaret Mead and the reclusive and lonely Ruth Benedict. Both were students of Franz Boas and both were responsible for popularizing his views. In *Malpsychia* Joyce Milton writes that Ruth Benedict and Margaret Mead began a clandestine love affair in the summer of 1923. Their academic fondness for uncorrupted primitive cultures was as intense as their licentious fondness for each other. After turning their backs on their respective husbands by pursuing a lesbian relationship, how hard could it be to turn their backs on the search for truth in advancing their defective theory of cultural relativism?

One doesn't have to be a psychoanalyst to see that Mead had transformed Ta'ū into her own personal Fantasy Island, a place where it was possible to experiment sexually without becoming entangled in the social and emotional repercussions that were making her own life so complicated (Milton, 28).

Although a distinction must be made between biography and ideas, that is to say — that the relationship is contingent — there is a criterion to judge the significance of the relationship. If the ideas are true, then biography is not significant except as biography. If the ideas are false and often deliberately false, as is the case with Mead, Freud, Reich, and Kinsey, then biography is significant in understanding the ideas.

Besides Mead's *Coming of Age in Samoa*, her *Growing Up in New Guinea* (1930) and her *Sex and Temperament in Three Primitive Societies* (1935) together with Ruth Benedict's *Patterns of Culture* (1934) provide readers with a little library of documents that popularized and advanced Boas' theory of cultural relativism and social determinism as well as being textbook cases of what sociologist, Steven Goldberg, calls "wish replac[ing] thought."

Wrapped in smirks, sneers, and snarls, there will be those who will say that this is old stuff, to which we reply, "the beat goes on." It can be heard in the songs sung by feminists about the brutality of men to their wives and girlfriends on Super Bowl Sunday; in the social and historical recreations (e.g., the TV show, *Roots,* 1977) promoted by the race commissars in show business; and in the fairytales told in the name of pseudo-tolerance to American school children after September 11, 2001 about the peaceful character of Islam. It reverberates in the suppression of the discovery of Kennewick man — a "forbidden discovery" as anthropologist Glynn Custred puts it in his essay for *Academic Questions,* Summer, 2000 (Custred, 12). The discovery, made in the state of Washington in 1996. appears to be a 9000 year old skeleton of a man "who looked more like a European accountant than he did a Paleoindian hunter" (Custred, 13). The meaning of the discovery suggests that there were European-like men in America before 1492 and earlier than "Native American" populations. Such a discovery is of course intolerable to politically correct social scientists and their clients in the American Indian Movement. The discovery must be suppressed by all means necessary and all means possible.

Humanistic Psychology as Mock Redemption

Humanistic psychology would soon add to the corrosive effects achieved by cultural relativism. Abraham Maslow, the inspiration, along with Marx, of Feminist Queen Bee, Betty Friedan, was himself influenced by Frankfurters, Marcuse, Reich, and Fromm in his theories of female dominance and self-actualization; female dominance not incidentally being a major feature of Babylonian fertility cults. As far as self-actualization is concerned, it is caught in the so very informative slogan: "Be all that you can be."

Abraham Maslow was a friend and a student of Ruth Benedict. His theory of personality, redefining normality, gave us the phrases "peak experience," "self-actualization," and "self-esteem." They are embedded in the language of today's therapeutic society. Maslow's hierarchy of needs is ranked in order, starting with the four basic needs; food and shelter; safety and security; love and acceptance; and success or recognition by others. After these basic needs are satisfied, the individual can begin the process of self-actualization. Anyone familiar with Aristotle's *Metaphysics* will recognize that Maslow's hierarchy of needs is a second-rate copy of Aristotle's contention that human beings in the quest for civilization pursue the necessities of life, then rest and recreation. Once these are secured and leisure obtained, they pursue theoretical knowledge in physics, mathematics, and finally philosophy.

Maslow's *Eupsychia* — his theoretical utopia of healthy psyches — is strikingly similar to Aristotle's *Eudaemonia* — a sense of material, psychological, and physical well-being achieved by pursuing all other goods in the right manner. Few critics of Maslow's theory note these similarities to Aristotle's thought — a further testament to the corruption of intellectual standards. Aristotle is concerned with the practical affairs of daily life and moral situations in pursuit of theoretical wisdom which is what defines human beings as human.

Maslow was dissatisfied with behaviorist psychology as well as with Freudian psychoanalysis. He theorized that infants would grow into unselfish caring adults if the four basic needs were satisfied. A mere two percent of all individuals would achieve self-actualization. His theory of self-actualization is based on biographical analyses of individuals he considered self-actualized. The list of these self-actualized individuals is little more than hagiography shrouded in pseudo-scientific jargon. Ironically, Maslow lists the lonely, troubled, and depressed Ruth Benedict as a self-actualized person. Is this science?

Carl Rogers takes humanistic psychology one step further. The therapist is now a "facilitator" and the patient solves his own problems. The Freudian "confessional" metastasized into reality television. Rogers promoted "feelings," "nurturing," "non-directive therapy," and "growth experiences," on the road to becoming fully human. The behaviorists would lead us to their utopia, *Walden Two*, by manipulating human behavior through operant conditioning; the humanist psychologists would lead us to *Eupsychia*, a fellowship of healthy psyches, by satisfying basic needs and preparing individuals for self-actualization. Rogers assured us that the road to becoming fully human required the removal of all forms of authority. Skinner's experiments with pigeons, Maslow's studies of monkeys and chimpanzees, and Rogers' "treatment" of dysfunctional personalities illuminated the yellow brick road to becoming "fully" human. A trusting public and an uncritical gang of intellectuals accepted this as "social science." In truth, it was little more than "K-Mart self-service psychoanalysis" featuring such weekly specials as "encounter groups," "T-groups," and other forms of non-judgmental therapy for "normals." The public lined up before the doors opened. The promise of being fully human clouded reason and throughout the Emerald City people forgot what every ordinarily intelligent person knows: being non-judgmental or non-directive is a deliberate decision; that is, a judgment.

To illustrate the destructive power of such bad ideas, consider Carl Rogers' work with a community of nuns. Rogers and William R. Coulson, a Roman Catholic graduate student at Notre Dame who wrote his thesis on Rogers' theory of human nature, directed the Education Innovation Project. This was a two year experiment involving the entire religious community of the Sisters of the Immaculate Heart of Mary located in Los Angeles. Students, teachers, nuns, and priests bared their innermost thoughts and feelings. Gratuitous assertions proclaiming self realizations were considered "growth signs" while doubt and reticence signaled refusal to "open up." Civilization's guardrails crumbled as participants explored strange and unknown feelings. Prayer, modesty, and community succumbed to sexual exploration, impulse, and intolerance. "Only by becoming comfortable with the dark side of the self could the individual hope to find his true identity and become 'real' in his relations to others" (Milton, 142). Within two years the community descended into chaos, and then it fell apart.

But this is not the end of the "story." Coulson had the decency to recognize the damage that he and Rogers wrought. He made acts of repentance and amendment by criticizing in lectures and articles the pernicious and destructive effects of manipulation employed to tear down the boundaries that make civilization possible. Not so, Rogers. Indeed his disciples and groupies by means of "sensitivity training," "encounter therapy," and "primal screams" continue to trash peoples' souls in the name of psychic health and liberation. Pushing the envelope? What trash! It is the stuff that nightmares are made of!

CHAPTER THREE:
Science and the Bad Ideas of Scientism

Wondrous Science

It would be the height of foolishness and the depth of ignorance, especially from the posture of dismissive ridicule, not to marvel and praise the accomplishments of the physical sciences as well as the technology which flows from them. We are not only talking about the accomplishments of modern science and technology but also those achieved in Ancient and Medieval times. When we speak about the physical sciences we mean physics, chemistry, biology, and their subdivisions. We do not regard mathematics as belonging to the category of the physical sciences. It is rather the language of the sciences. As such, mathematics fits better into the medieval classification as part of the liberal arts, that is, as part of the Quadrivium which includes arithmetic, geometry, astronomy and music. The reason for the better fit is that, as the language of the sciences, mathematics certifies and makes precise the conduct of the sciences. It can, however, be understood as a science in the ancient and medieval sense as the philosophic investigation of the nature of number and quantity. The modern sense extends that investigation to include the nature of relationship in general. In the modern sense too, there arises the issue of whether mathematical relations are discoveries or inventions — an issue that did not arise in Ancient and Medieval mathematics; both of which maintained that they are discoveries.

The accomplishments of science must be understood in two senses: the first is the theoretical sense which begins in wonder and curiosity, then attempts to explain the world in terms of its existence, its structure and order, and its relation to space and time. Science does so through observation, experimentation, formulation of theories and laws in order to discover facts about things and then to explain the "how" and "why" of things. This is done not just to discover the "how," as we are told by the dogmatists, but the "why" as well: for the "how" of things cannot be explained without reference to the "why" of things. In this first theoretical sense the things of the world are uncovered and discovered for the sake of knowing and understanding them — for the joy of standing before the truth of things, as the more refined Brooklyn Existentialists would put it.

The second sense has to do with the application of the facts, principles and explanations in order to have some control or dominion over the world — conquest is too strong a term for that control — by means of technology. This is the practical side of the sciences, that is, the inventing of tools to build, to travel, to communicate and, in general, to make human life a little more pleasing or at least more bearable. These tools, in turn, make possible even more knowledge about the material world so as to enable the human animal to act as producer, reproducer and custodian. To object to technology because of its abuse is no argument against technology itself but against its abuse. The abuse can and will occur because of human fallibility and imperfectability. Recourse to law and punishment of abusers will not do, since law professors have corrupted law to the point that they say punishment has nothing to do with justice. Indeed they even say that law has nothing to do with justice (e.g., Hans Kelsen and Oliver Wendell Holmes, Jr.). But more about this later. We would like to say that natural justice should be left to the tender ministrations of Vinny the Fish, Tony Baccala or Nicky-No-Neck but that too would play to the Principalities and Powers of this world who celebrate and encourage such criminal types. We prefer to say as consistent Brooklyn Existentialists, that the abusers are to be left to Heaven.

To return now to the relationship of the practical second sense of science to the theoretical first sense, we offer some examples. There is the relationship of dependence between all kinds of engineering to the principles of physics, that of the art of medicine on the science of biology, and that of prescribing the use of medicines or drugs on the science of chemistry. Only a fool, an idiot, or a nihilist, who is both, could not wonder at and appreciate the successes of the physical sciences. But bad ideas hover around and trade on those successes. And only a fool, an idiot, or a nihilist would deny the tragic consequences of those successes. It is a tragedy taught so strikingly in the story of Frankenstein, the scientist, whose monster, born of science and technology, destroys him, what he loves, and those around him. The rest of this chapter will be devoted to a discussion of some of those bad ideas.

Science and Religion

One is the purported but false opposition and conflict between science and religion. This bad idea was not always so. In the science of the Pythagoreans (6th Century B.C.) and of Plato, it was not so. The Pythagoreans were a religious brotherhood of astronomer-mathematicians who sought and discovered a divine order in the mathematical character of nature. It was the intelligibility of that divine order that they found and venerated by way of and in the mathematical relations that bound together everything else in nature. Number and geometric form could be applied to anything and everything because nature itself had numerical and geometric structure. Mathematics was the very form and foundation of things. This was the metaphysical truth for the Pythagoreans. It was a scientific and religious truth as well.

The Pythagoreans can and have been criticized (by Plato and Aristotle among others) for taking *a* truth about nature for the whole truth or even the most basic truth, inasmuch as nature shows itself to be more than basically mathematical. Nevertheless there is no doubt that for the Pythagoreans, religion and science were not in conflict. Both bespoke the divine harmony of nature and of their harmony with each other.

For Plato, moreover, the distinction between myth or poetry (*mythos*) and reason or science (*logos*) was not an opposition such that one would have to choose between them, as Nietzsche chose myth and Darwin chose science. The relationship was complementary. Myths are imaginative representations of the forces and elements of nature. They embody truths best told and easily understood (and not only for children) in the form of stories. Their rhetorical and pedagogical value does not negate their logical and scientific value as stories bearing truths that are to be interpreted and explained. One dialogue, but not the only one, in which Plato accounts for the complementarity is the *Timaeus*. Plato was not a demythologizer as some Biblical exegetes have been in their efforts to jettison myths as childish and superstitious in the name of science, history, and truth. The only myths Plato would have jettisoned are "myths" in the journalistic sense of lies and pure fiction. His so-called "noble lie" is not pure fiction but a pragmatic truth of political thinking intended to instruct citizens of republics to be wary of utopias on one hand and to act honorably on the other.

To be honest about the Ancient World and its understanding of the relationship between religion and science, it is necessary to report the minority view of the Atomists and the Epicureans. Their view of science was that it was incompatible with religion. The gods do not exist; death is ceasing to be; pleasure is the only good and pain the only evil.

In the Medieval Era science was pursued and done in monasteries and in universities, the latter being institutions which were founded in and are characteristic of the period. From this fact one could hardly expect to find a conflict between science and religion. The religious orders of the Benedictines, the Franciscans, and the Dominicans who worked in the monasteries or staffed the universities had no problem unifying their scientific studies with their religious lives because they took philosophy seriously and because the founder of their religion declared himself to be "the way, the truth, and the life." This is not to say that they had no problems, but a conflict between science and religion was not one of them. The sciences were thought to be capable of finding the signs and traces of the Divine in nature. The search was not by way of Cabalistic secret doctrines, alchemy, or shall we say, voodoo science, although that sort of stuff was around in the Middle Ages. Science was done by way of observing, describing, and explaining nature, and, if possible, predicting its course.

The issue of the opposition between religion and science is also known as the faith versus reason controversy which is the formulation it took during and after the Protestant revolt in the 16th century. Faith was regarded as the posture of the sovereign individual Christian before the Biblical revelation of God's activity and human duty with respect to that activity. Man's duty was to hear God's word and obey His will in order to achieve salvation from sin. The posture of reason, by contrast, was frequently regarded as idolatrous and in no way a path to God. It had been and is corrupted by sin. Faith alone saves.

The 18th century Enlightenment accepted the radical separation between the two postures, then confidently shoved aside the posture and content of faith as unenlightened, superstitious and the main cause of political discord, something which became hideously evident in the Thirty Years War (1618-1648). It is to the Enlightenment that we owe the current view of the separation between faith and reason — a view which has its partisans among Biblical fundamentalists and agnostic or atheistic scientists and philosophers.

Athens and Jerusalem

The separation is a perennially bad idea even in its jazzy formulation by Tertullian, an African Father of the Church (c. 155-220 A.D). He puts it this way. "What indeed has Athens to do with Jerusalem?" (*On the Prescription of Heretics*, 7, 3). With Athens standing for reason and Jerusalem for faith, then, for Tertullian — nothing! He taught that whatever hints of truth there may be in the thoughts of the philosophers were stolen from Biblical revelation whether the philosophers had read the Bible or not. With thoughts like that, it is no surprise that he ended his life in the heresy of Montanism which taught, among other things, a moral rigorism — a holier-than-thou-ism, to which New

England Puritanism subscribed only too faithfully. The Church taught and argued exactly the opposite of this bad idea (that reason and faith have nothing to do with each other) even into our own time, especially in the Papal Encyclical *Fides et Ratio* (Faith and Reason), 1998.

There is another way to understand the opposition of Athens to Jerusalem. It is the way of Leo Strauss who has influenced a good number of American political philosophers primarily, then political scientists, then politicians. Among those influenced are some Brooklyn Existentialists — but not of the Frenchy kind. Strauss' way of regarding the opposition is with a kind of Talmudic "on one hand; on the other hand" treatment. He understands the tension between reason and revelation, the secret of which is that the ambiguity must be permanent. For Strauss, religion is not merely an instrument to preserve moral and political order.

Maimonides, revered by Thomas Aquinas as Rabbi Moses, held that faith and reason were compatible. Any apparent conflict between the two comes from a misreading of either the philosophers or Scripture or both. The issue then becomes one of the authoritative reading to judge the misreadings.

In Catholic thought the recent Papal Encyclical *Fides et Ratio*, drawing primarily on Thomas Aquinas, affirms and declares the public character of truth and the complementary nature of reason and faith, of science and religion, of philosophy and revelation. This has to be so for Catholics since Jesus is the Logos, the Word of God. Consequently, Catholics say that the tension and separation between Athens and Jerusalem are reconciled in Rome. And Rome says that, contrary to Tertullian and his fellow separatists in the course of history, Athens has everything to do with Jerusalem. Reason and faith meet in Rome's conception of that relationship not as mere assertion, that is, not because Rome says so but as reasoned argument. Faith is not "a leap into the absurd," as Soren Kierkegaard says, and his thoughtless mimics repeat because, we suppose, the pronouncement has a dramatic character. But this pronouncement relegates religion to the domain of the absurd. It dismisses the continuity between reason and faith. The domain of faith is not the domain of unreason, i.e., of the absurd. Rather, faith is the posture of wanting to know more, to know what one does not know. Faith is the complement of reason in the pursuit of knowledge and the acknowledgment of reason's finitude. The complementarity applies to the other formulations of this issue, as well, i.e., to science and religion, to philosophy and revelation. Science and philosophy attend to the natural order while religion and revelation transcend the natural order.

The argument begins, and here we will give it the Brooklyn Existentialist touch, with two common sense empirical propositions. The first is the mind's capacity for meaning and truth; the second is the human desire for them. Science (including philosophy) and religion are two sources of meaning and truth. And meaning and truth are the tests or criteria for both sources. The opposition between them is a false opposition — a false disjunction, as the logic textbooks put it, if one understands the territory of each and the common ground between them. They are distinct but not separate. If the opposition is absolute, then common or public knowledge and truth are not possible. Of course, there will always be those jokers who go around saying that there is no meaning and no truth. "Nobody ever understands anything." "Nobody ever finds anything out." The chorus from the stoop hollers: "What do you mean?" "Are those statements true?" "You do want those statements to be true, don't you?" Then there are those other kinds of jokers who say that they don't want truth — don't care for it. They just want pleasure. To which the voices from the stoop urge sardonically: "Whatever gives you pleasure or whatever your impulse or whim, you go for it or go do it. And we mean whatever! Then make sure that nobody else finds out — if you can."

The belief that you could separate religion from science or faith from reason was named "Averroism" in the Middle Ages after Averroes, the Islamic philosopher and a commentator on Aristotle's philosophy. Disputing with other Islamic philosophers such as Avicenna and al Farabi, he tried to separate philosophy and science from religion. Against the Islamic theologian, al

Ghazzali, he tried to defend philosophy itself. His solution was the trap of the theory of "double truth." Islamic thinkers are susceptible to this bad idea, as are literalists, be they in religion or in science. Most Protestants are susceptible. The very influential German Protestant philosopher, Immanuel Kant, even proposed a philosophical proof against common sense for his version of the separation of faith and reason in his *Critique of Pure Reason* (1787).

So what's the story here? The story is that meaning and truth in science are one thing while meaning and truth in religion are another. What has meaning or is true in science does not have meaning or is true in religion and vice-versa. In trying to preserve both domains in their absolute separation, the believers in this bad idea are led to the fallacy of either science or religion but not both. Or they are led to the less common but nonetheless equivalent fallacy of neither science nor religion. It is less common because to hold that neither science nor religion are true, one would have to be a skeptic, a cynic, and a nihilist all wrapped up in one package. Both fallacies say that there is no common knowledge and no truth. Another way to put it is to say that the meaning of truth is not one. This is both a bad idea and, of course, false. There are many opinions that can be true or false; there are many truths and there are many truths about one thing. But the meaning of truth is one, i.e., truth is disclosure of things such that it is possible to say what is the case and what is not the case.

Consequently, it is true to say that science and religion are distinct. They are, for example, distinct in their methods and language. But they are not separate in knowledge, united as they are in their beginnings in ordinary experience and united as they are in the ends of knowledge — to understand nature as a whole and in its particulars.

Scientism

It is ironic that the historical event most often cited to illustrate how religion impedes the advance of science is the trial of Galileo. The irony is that at the time of the trial, the philosophy of nature, which we now call science, had not yet been divorced from faith. The circumstances of the trial are more often exaggerated than retold accurately in order to create the popular belief that science stands for truth and knowledge whereas faith stands for superstition and credulity. This maleducated view of the relationship between science and religion had not yet taken hold at the time of the trial. The originality in the observations of Copernicus, Kepler, Galileo and Newton sought to understand nature, not to tinker with it. Their creativity in astronomy and cosmology unsettled medieval popular belief and laid the foundation for what would become the modern scientific revolution. Yet they were cautious in proclaiming their discoveries; for they understood that scientific discoveries had religious and political implications. They had not yet reduced nature to indiscreet bundles of brute matter. They did not divorce faith from reason, religion from science.

We have forgotten, or never knew, what the Pythagorean Brotherhood exemplified — an organic society united in goals and interests within an organic nature; vital and not artificial. The enlightened, modern pronouncement that science is "progressive" is metaphysical baggage insinuated into the conversation to demean religion and to mislead an unsuspecting and uninformed public. The cheerleading about progress masks the fact that discoveries in the physical sciences are often accidental breakthroughs which advance along nonlinear paths and frequently bewilder their discoverers. The contemporary caricature of the modern scientist as a pure rational agent in pursuit of the truth, free from prejudices, political biases, and philosophical dispositions is contrasted with the religious fundamentalist who reads the Bible literalistically. Recall the portrayals of the antagonists on the issue of teaching evolution in the movie *Inherit the Wind* (Stanley Kramer, 1960).

For two centuries the charade has worked. But science ceases to be science when it fails to understand its limitations. Nietzsche's stunning pronouncement that "God is dead" assured intellectuals that God no longer is a player in the marketplace of ideas. Colleges and universities ceased to be the abode of the arts and sciences and became the seminaries of antihuman secularism, politically correct dogmas, and nihilistic irrationalism. Moral obligations were, at best, illusory. Although Copernicus thought the earth was not the center of the universe, he never believed that man was. Scientists of modernity absorbed the enthusiasm and fanaticism of religious fundamentalists in their overreaching claims. Freud reduced human nature to irrational and unconscious desires. Edward O. Wilson and Richard Dawkins, in advancing Darwinism, reduced human beings to products of genetic random mutations. B. F. Skinner reduced human behavior to operant conditioning insisting that human consciousness was irrelevant and not measurable. Was he conscious when he said that? And, by the way, it is measurable in and by human actions and products. These examples illustrate what we mean by scientism; that is, the reductionism that results when scientists exaggerate or extend their observations and explanations beyond the limits of their respective disciplines. In other words, scientism says that there is no knowledge outside of science. It is when science no longer distinguishes between metaphysical presuppositions and evidence that it ceases to be science and becomes dogma. The fact that the history of science is littered with erroneous theories once believed to be true is recognized and then forgotten by many scientists. We need only mention the theories of heliocentrism and phlogiston. Ignoring such errors, the so-called empiricist, that is, the scientist, becomes a fanatical dogmatist, that is, a "scientista." The scientist observes, explains, and predicts. The "scientista" insists, advocates, and defends the canon. For example, Darwinists know that "random mutation" cannot explain the "irreducible complexity" of organisms. But they also know that without random mutation, Darwinism, not evolution, is a theory in trouble. Random mutation, like "instinct" in biology, is a magic trick to misinform a trusting public. We really cannot explain "how" these behaviors occur, so let's make up a word or phrase.

Among the "sophisticated" Darwinists there is an open admission that a teleological order exists in nature. Ordinary folks these days get to know this by watching nature programs on TV when they are informed that in the struggle for survival, eyes are for seeing, hands and claws are for grasping and that the beaks of finches in the Galapagos Islands grow or diminish according to the character of the food supply. Evolution and design are compatible. Both are observable. Both are scientific. What the "sophisticated" Darwinists add to the equation is that the goal directed order in nature is the result of natural selection understood as the random and mechanistic play of elementary material particles over long periods of time or over shorter periods of time, depending on the Darwinists you consult.

Randomness, however, begets randomness — without a principle of order in the "primordial soup." The hypothesis that randomness, of itself, generating nature's ordered complexity, does not even rise to the level of logical possibility, let alone physical possibility. The physical possibility of generating nature's complexity had to have been already present in the "soup." If, moreover, natural selection is the designer principle, then *a fortiori*, you have design. Insisting that the cause of design, i.e., natural selection, is completely random, is gratuitous, unscientific, illogical and in bad faith.

The dogmatists reject even the possibility that the intelligibility of nature requires an intelligence or formative principle as part of the explanation, despite the fact that their own actions imply order and purpose. However, to reason in this way keeps people in their proper place, ignorant and manipulable. "Enlightenment" science demands that theology and physics must be kept apart, with theology being relegated to fairytales. Such are the effects of scientism.

When change occurs in science, it is heralded as a triumph. When Einstein developed his theory of relativity, scientists did not claim that Newtonian physics had been defeated. The new theory was understood as an advance not as a defeat of the old. Religion, on the other hand, always suffers defeat as new scientific theories are advanced because it is regarded as a rival for knowledge not a partner. Recalling Pope Urban VIII's argument made to Galileo, Arthur Koestler writes "that a hypothesis which works must not necessarily have anything to do with reality for there may be alternative explanations of how the

Lord Almighty produces the phenomenon in question. If there is a lesson in our story it is that the manipulation, according to strictly self-consistent rules, of a set of symbols representing one single aspect of the phenomena may produce correct, verifiable predictions, and yet completely ignore all other aspects whose ensemble constitutes reality" (*Sleepwalkers*, 542-533). What Koestler criticizes is the view that the conceptual systems of science, mathematics, and theoretical physics are closed because the terms and ideas within the respective systems are defined in terms of one another. The mathematical equations and formulations that unify the abstractions within these scientific systems are not synonymous with real "things." For example, the book which you presently hold in your hand and are reading is a solid thing, yet we are told by science that it is mostly empty space when we consider its molecular composition and the dimensions of its subatomic particles.

Goodbye to Common Sense

To say that solid things are really mostly empty space and to say that despite appearances everything really exists as just a random play of lifeless particles is supposed to assert profound scientific truths. This, say the scientistas, is the way things are. As we "scientists" have done, so too you must tear away the veil of illusion woven by common sense and common perception. Saying the first blurs the real differences between solids, liquids and gases. Among other things, such statements are an attempt to appear profound about the real status of things. Together with the second statement it plays into the presuppositions of mechanistic materialism which is not a scientific doctrine at all but a metaphysical doctrine — a doctrine which is both a presupposition and one that is highly dubious at that.

Mechanistic materialism affirms that only matter exists beneath the surface of the complexity and diversity of things. The fact that no one has ever come across matter as such eludes the materialist. What one does come across is matter in the form of a multiplicity and variety of things. Atomic and sub-atomic particles, if they are not theoretical constructs, are matter in some form, behaving each in its own way. If we wanted to make a joke, caricature though it be, of the assertion that solids are mostly empty space, we could offer its proponents a practical test of such an assertion by suggesting that they jump in front of the "A" train when it pulls in the Jay Street – Borough Hall station in Brooklyn. If matter is mostly empty space, the scientistas are mostly empty headed. Caricature aside, the mechanistic part of the doctrine says that the way matter exists is, repeating what we said before, as a random play of lifeless particles beneath the order and variety of such things in the world as "lions and tigers and bears, as well as shoes and ships and sealing wax, of cabbages and kings." The motion of those lifeless particles, according to the mechanistic materialist, and despite appearances to the contrary, is just a random rubbing and bumping (night and day) against each other. Structure, order, form and mind do not really exist. They are the mere stink arising from mechanistic matter. Biology is reduced to chemistry and chemistry to a formless and orderless physics masquerading in mathematical costumes.

More recent theories in physics are not an improvement in scientific explanation. The String Theory of the character of matter and energy even when complemented by the Membrane Theory fails to explain the nature of the universe (or multiverse) and to predict its (or their) course. The strings or membranes of matter and energy are such that there is no way to observe them or even to demonstrate their existence. Nor do the theories make predictions that can be tested, verified, confirmed or falsified.

Two recent books in theoretical physics suggest that String-Membrane theory will go the way of the ether and phlogiston theories into the graveyard of scientific failures. One book is *The Trouble with Physics: The Rise of String Theory, the Fall of a Science and What Comes Next* (2006) by Lee Smolin. The other is *Not Even Wrong: The Failure of String Theory and the Search for Unity in Physical Law* (2006) by Peter Woit. Both authors are theoretical physicists whose skepticism about String-Membrane theory as a "theory of everything" suggests something beyond mere failure to the Existentialists from Brooklyn. In their search for a theory of everything in science, physicists drift into the region of metaphysics. As a result, they are faced with a choice. They can do physics within a sound metaphysics or stick to a physics that explains and predicts without embracing a gratuitous metaphysics such as materialism. The watchword is finitude.

Let's take another bad idea of the scientistas. They say glibly but with willful ignorance that intelligent, and therefore intelligible, design in nature is a religious doctrine and thereby to be dismissed as having no scientific character. In fact it was a philosophic and scientific doctrine of the Ancient world. So far as we know, among the first thinkers to formulate it was Anaxagoras who said that *Nous* (Mind) set all things in order. Heraclitus gave the name *Logos* (Reason) to the principle of order in an ever changing world. We have already mentioned the Pythagoreans whose take on order was that it was mathematical. But it was Aristotle who gave the most complete form of this account in both his Physics and Metaphysics. That things act for an end or goal in nature is, for Aristotle, a scientific description. He argues that the general design or order (acting for an end) observable in the diversity and complexity of nature leads to the further scientific inquiry about the *specific* explanation, the specific order for individuals and species. Since science is part of philosophy for Aristotle, then intelligent design, another name for the teleological order in nature, is philosophical as well as scientific but *not* religious. For Aristotle and in truth, however, knowledge is not such that whatever is not science is religious. And whatever is religious is non-cognitive or emotive or both. His arguments have indeed been used by theologians to think about a creator God, but Aristotle himself did not conceive of a creator God. His idea of a Prime Mover is not a creator God. One can discover design and order without conceiving of a creator God. We should add here a caution about Aristotle's errors in astronomy and physics not counting against all his work. We certainly don't discard Einstein's general theory or relativity because he abandoned his concept of a "cosmological constant" when later discoveries refuted a stationary universe.

Without the *prima facie* observation of design and order, there is no possibility of even beginning a scientific account of things through description, explanation and formulation of laws. While the scientists pretend to dismiss design and order, their very attempts to explain nature surreptitiously presuppose that order, rightly so this time.

How could people like David Hume and his like-minded skeptical twerps (we don't mean that in a bad way) talk about the regularity of nature without knowing that regularity implies order! The exceptions to the order do show that the order is not perfect or infallible, not that there is no rule or order.

While we are at it, that is, talking about cosmology, we are going to bring up the topic of "the flat earth" which the scientistas use as a straw man to club the benighted science of the Ancient and Medieval eras. In the first place the sphericity of the earth was known in the Ancient world by the Pythagoreans, in particular Aristarchus of Samos, an astronomer of the third century B.C. He discovered such truths not by sense perception, although beginning with it, but by mathematical calculations. Renaissance astronomers such as Copernicus did not rediscover this lost knowledge for about 1700 years. We can pine about what might have been, had the library at Alexandria which contained ancient writings not been burned.

The proof, moreover, that medieval scholars knew about the sphericity of the earth was the concept of the Orbis Terrarum (Surround or globe of the earth). This concept of the planet was known and used in the medieval universities, the recognition of which by serious thinkers should dispel (but it won't) the purportedly Medieval concept of a flat earth. It won't because there is a lot at stake for the scientistas in keeping this bad idea around. Remember for them the word and era, Medieval, means unenlightened and bad. Modern means enlightened and good.

Although the earth is a sphere and revolves around the sun, it does not look that way. Except for satellite photos, no one located at any spot on the earth could see the earth's sphericity. From any spot on earth, the earth looks flat. Because of this, and unless people have access to satellite photos which show its sphericity and curvature, they would believe that the earth is flat, because it looks that way. As far as seeing the earth revolving around the sun, one would have to do so from a perspective in space to observe the relation of both bodies to each other. As we pointed out earlier, the knowledge that the earth is spherical and that it revolves around the sun, not the other way round, was arrived at by mathematical calculation in combination with perception long before space travel and satellite photos. As a result, we still say the sun rises and sets not because it does so but because it looks so. Consequently, it is true to say that the earth looks flat and that the sun looks as if it rises and sets. It is false to say that they are true but not false to say that they seem true.

The difference between the way things look and the way they are has led some scientists and philosophers such as Rene Descartes and Immanuel Kant to reject common perception and common sense for "scientific" thinking. Of course, serious scientists cannot reject either. Those that do, do it in their bad hypothetical moments. They cannot do so indefinitely unless they are ideological jerks. For what is it that tests hypotheses, confirms theories, learns from experience and verifies predictions except repeatable common perceptions? And what is it that distinguishes good ideas from bad ideas, authentic scientists from scientistas, if not critical common sense?

Just the Facts, Ma'am

Another form of the radical separation between religion and science can be found in the "fact-value" distinction, a concept developed to distinguish statements about what "is" from statements about what "ought" to be. Statements about what is are "facts" and are scientific and verifiable. Statements about what "ought" to be are expressions of value and simply represent what others have agreed to and feel about things. Year after year, students are told that water is a molecule made up of two hydrogen atoms and one oxygen atom. That's a fact! In this way, they are exposed to an uncritical acceptance of the fact-value distinction. What they are not told is that to consider the molecular composition of water implies the acceptance of the "value" that we can understand real things scientifically. The radicalized fact-value debate simply begs the question that the fact-value distinction intends to clarify. For those not preoccupied with the scientific value of water, it can be a cooling and refreshing drink on a hot afternoon as well as the sacramental substance in the ritual of baptism.

In its radical expression, the fact-value distinction claims that normative statements are not grounded in statements of fact. The only authentic knowledge is scientific knowledge. Statements in religion, ethics, and metaphysics are devoid of cognitive meaning and represent mere opinion. Imagine for the moment that a Logical Positivist on trial for murder has been convicted based on a preponderance of the evidence (the standard applied in the practice of civil and criminal law). Rising in protest, his defense attorney appeals to the judge and the jury and argues that the verdict is nonsense since no one can derive a normative decision from statements of fact. Although the verdict may be in error, the practice of law presupposes that decisions and judgments can be and are made on the basis of facts. In the case of civil and criminal law, "justice" is not meaningless. Better yet is the status of the organism in the monumental abortion controversy. Is it an undeveloped fetus or an unborn child? It is in fact both an undeveloped fetus and an unborn human child. Whatever it is, the fact determines what ought to be and ought not to be done.

Many who advocate a radical separation between statements of fact and statements of value rely on the "verifiability principle" of meaning; that is, statements of fact can be tested as to their truth or falsity. Critics of this criterion of meaning correctly point out that the principle itself is not verifiable. It is the principle or standard of meaning and beyond the reach of empirical testing. The principle of verification is a philosophical statement of science and as such it "transcends" the form and content of logical and empirical statements. You might even say that the principle of verification is a "first principle" or metaphysical statement. As a result, the radical separation between statements of fact and statements of value rebounds on itself. For example, a radical empiricist can claim that statements such as "1 + 1 = 2" or "Ebbet's Field was located in Brooklyn" have meaning. A Brooklyn Existentialist would then ask, "What is the meaning of meaning?" The claim that "a statement has meaning" is beyond the content and substance of the statement and, we would add, metaphysical. A "logical" logical positivist or radical empiricist could state that "Ebbet's Field was located in Brooklyn" or "1 + 1=2" and even claim these statements can be verified but must be silent as to whether these statements have meaning. Since you cannot verify the verification principle, it is not a statement of fact. But then what is it? A statement of value? If so, it is a nonsense statement. Q.E.D: the radical separation of facts and values is based on nonsense. For critical common sense realists, there is and has always been a harmony between statements of fact and statements of value. They know what Aristotle knew, "Human beings desire to know" and knowing the truth about things is good.

Karl Popper criticized the verifiability principle and offered an alternative in defining scientific statements in terms of falsifiabilty. For Popper, a statement or theory is scientific if it is falsifiable. Unlike the positivists, he did not claim that statements of religion, ethics, and metaphysics were meaningless. Popper was critical of traditional empirical methods in that they relied on observation and induction. He argued that science does not advance by finding instances which confirm hypotheses but by falsifying them. The instances of confirmation which occur when attempts are made to falsify a particular conjecture simply add to its "corroboration." Popper introduces the word "corroboration" to mean essentially what the word induction has always meant. Popper renames something already known and better said and claims to be saying something new. (A British knight should know better). For common sense realists, most scientists, and ordinary people, science works by induction, that is, through confirmation of hypotheses and conjectures. Furthermore, as Martin Gardner points out in his essay, "A Skeptical Look at Karl Popper," Popper realized every falsification of a conjecture is a confirmation of an opposite conjecture and vice versa but simply dismissed it as unimportant. Through such rhetorical magic tricks, Popper parlayed the standard textbook argument of the "counterexample" into a professional career.

To illustrate his exploitation of the counter example, consider the statement "All ravens are black." Popper argued that such a statement cannot be verified by repeated observations of countless black ravens; however the appearance of one raven of any other color is sufficient to falsify it. A statement that is consistent with every actual or possible observation is unfalsifiable and therefore unscientific. (The irrationalism implied by such convoluted use of logic and language may make sense to academics, but for common sense realists it is unintelligible.) Now consider Newton's first law of motion, namely, every object in a state of motion tends to remain in that state of motion unless an external force is applied to it. What are we to make of an object in motion that violates Newton's first law? Such objects must exist, at least potentially, for the law to be falsifiable and thus scientific. You must be very learned indeed to understand this bad idea.

What is uncommonly nonsensical in this Popperite definition of scientific statements is his assault on induction and the role of probability as science proceeds from observation and experiment to theory. Induction is the process of reasoning from particular observations and cases to general conclusions about those observations and cases. For Karl and the scientista Popperazzi who followed, science need not rely on induction; science is deductive and advances hypotheses which it then seeks to refute. Popper's enthusiasm for irrationality was absorbed by those who came after him. For example, Thomas Kuhn (*The Structure of Scientific Revolutions*, 1962) discovered "paradigm shifts" in the history of science. Knowledge, discovery, truth, and falsity are simply epiphenomena relative to a particular paradigm and represent the language used by advocates of the paradigm. Kuhn conflates history, sociology, and psychology with the philosophy of science to produce his hyperbolic relativism. The height of absurdity is reached by Paul K. Feyerabend (*Against Method*, 1975) when he suggests neither induction nor deduction as the method of empirical science, but rather, democratic voting to establish scientific laws. Feyerabend informs us that the only principle that will not inhibit the progress of science is "anything goes" — including things like witchcraft and voodoo. We are not surprised by these nonsensical and absurd ideas; for what is to be expected when you insist that science does not rely on induction. Reasonable people know that there is much truth, occasional falsity, and many successes in the progress of science. In fact, the history of Western science is basically a success story.

Tricksters, Charlatans, and Crackpots

There is something more that must be mentioned in our account of the physical sciences. Some scientists in the pursuit of discovery or invention commit fraud for the purpose of money, ideology, or glory — or all three. The scientistas are those who do it. Scientists, whatever their personal faults may be, do not. The events are rare but they do occur and those occurrences are noteworthy. The lure of government or foundation funding is, as the social scientist say, "correlated" with the fraud. As if calling it correlation excuses the misbehavior. Correlation is the "abracadabra" to misdirect a trusting public. Making the rounds through the corridors of science is the cynical comment that "science is what gets funded."

From students sabotaging other students' experiments in college or university laboratories to world-renowned scientists making false claims for their work, moral imperfectability (or original sin) gets a boost of verifiability. The recent (2006) case of Korean biologist, Hwang Woo Suk, is an instance. He falsely claimed to have created stem cells from cloned human embryos. Aside from the research itself being morally and legally controversial, Suk's purported results were fraudulent.

An even more recent case of deception and attempted fraud is that of a company, Advanced Cell Technology Inc. After issuing a news release (August 23, 2006) reporting that it produced embryonic stem cells "using an approach that does not harm embryos," the company's stock rose dramatically. When critics of the "approach" raised objections, the company admitted that all of the embryos were killed in the experiments, the results of which were originally published in the British journal, *Nature*. William Caldwell, the CEO of the company, replied that "[we] did not put out anything misleading." He added that the techniques of removing individual cells from embryos is used in a different field – diagnostic testing without harm to the embryos. Thanks for the irrelevancy.

Ruth Francis, a "spokesperson" for *Nature* , attributes "the problem' to short editorial staffing which "ended up with communication problems," excuses given for deception and incompetence.

Robert Lanza, M.D. and vice president of research said in the initial press release, which stimulated investor interest, public interest and media interest in the project, that its success "takes away the president's [i.e. Bush] last excuse to oppose the research" (*Wall Street Journal*, 9/1/06). The *Wall Street Journal* then reported the baffling assertion that the company did not do the experiment that whipped up the media attention. If the experiment wasn't even done, then how can there be any talk about extracting cells and harming or not harming the embryos? (9/5/06, p. A19). The deceptions continue.

Caldwell, Francis, and Lanza have earned the right to be full-fledged scientistas.

Ernst Haeckel's drawings of early vertebrate embryos to illustrate the idea of a common ancestor for organisms in the Darwinian theory of evolution are more notorious. The drawings found their way into biology textbooks and have been taught by teachers for a long time now. Despite their exposures as frauds, they continue to be taught and defended in such textbooks as Douglas Futuyma's *Evolution* (2005). To his credit, Stephen J. Gould called the drawings "frauds" (*Natural History*, March, 2000).

Finally, the need for a missing link between apes and humans motivated the Piltdown fraud. Arthur Smith Woodward reconstructed an entire skull from the fossils discovered by amateur paleontologist Charles Dawson. The Piltdown specimen confirmed ideological commitment to evolutionary theory and influenced how fossils were interpreted for decades. The little skepticism that existed in 1912 was quickly overshadowed by how well the Piltdown specimen fit the prediction that human ancestors would have large skulls and ape-like jaws. After some forty years, scientists concluded that Piltdown man was a fraud. Scientists demonstrated that the Piltdown skull belonged to a modern human and the jaw fragment belonged to a modern orangutan. Furthermore, the jaw had been chemically treated and its teeth filed. "But the more interesting lesson to be learned from Piltdown," according to Jonathan Wells in *Icons of Evolution*, (2000) "is that scientists, like everyone else, can be fooled into seeing what they want to see" (Wells, 218).

Double Helix – Double Cross

The case against James Watson deserves special treatment for its success in misdirection, not quite reaching the level of fraud. His "sleight of word and deed" would culminate in Nobel Prizes for himself and his accomplices Francis Crick and Maurice Wilkens. The careful reader will note the absence of any mention of Rosalind Franklin, the "mark" in the great DNA string. The history of science memorializes the accomplishment of Watson and Crick as the discovery of the "the double helix," but critical common sense realists know it to be a caricature of the modern scientist as a pure rational agent in pursuit of the truth.

In *The Double Helix* Watson describes Rosalind Franklin as a "competent" although "ineffective" scientist who could not interpret her own data. In his "personal account of the discovery of the structure of DNA" he refers to her as "Rosy" — "a nickname never used by any friend of Rosalind's," according to Anne Sayre in her biography of Rosalind Franklin entitled *Rosalind Franklin and DNA* (Sayre, 19). By calling her "Rosy," Watson creates a character, in the way writers create characters in short stories and novels, to be handled as he chooses. In the case of Rosalind Franklin, Watson's literary license misrepresented a creative, energetic, brilliant young scientist whose contributions were essential in discovering the structure of DNA. Her diffraction photograph #51 showed the clearest evidence of a helical structure for DNA. Maurice Wilkens showed this photograph to Watson without Rosalind's consent. Franklin's quantitative data discussing the placement of phosphates in the DNA model were given to Francis Crick by Max Perutz, Crick's thesis adviser. Voilà, Watson and Crick come up with the structure of DNA. In 1962 Watson, Crick, and Wilkens received the Nobel Prize for "their" work on the structure of DNA. Only Wilkens mentioned her by name in accepting his prize. Rosalind Franklin could not correct their omissions because she died of cancer in 1958. These "gentlemen" of science behaved rather curiously in the case of Rosalind Franklin. Alas, ambition trumps truth and morality in this brave new world of science.

The Double Helix remains a supplemental text to a wide variety of science courses. We recommend that it be listed with an asterisk in the way Roger Maris' "61" homeruns in 1961 is listed in baseball history. Whether the legacy of Rosalind Franklin will be restored or not is a matter for future generations to decide. Our account of the double helix double cross ends with the words Aaron Klug spoke in tribute to Rosalind Franklin, "What she touched, she adorned" (Sayre, 181).

The Twilight Zone

Francis Crick is a telling example of what Socrates says to the Athenians in Plato's Apology about the skilled craftsman:

> *They understood things which I did not and to that extent, they*
> *were wiser than I was. But, gentlemen, these professional experts*

seem to share the same failing which I had noticed in the poets. I mean that on the strength of their technical proficiency they claimed a perfect understanding of every subject, however important, and I felt that this error more than outweighed their positive wisdom (Apology, 22d).

Take for instance the title of one of Crick's books, *The Astonishing Hypothesis: The Scientific Search for the Soul.* It commits such a blatant category mistake that the title and the thesis are ridiculous. Science does not search for the soul. It observes, describes, and formulates theories that attempt to explain the things in the observable universe. The soul does not come under the category of observable things. It is not a body such that it can be treated as the subject of a scientific search in the conventional sense.

Furthermore, when Crick says in that same work that "[t]he Astonishing Hypothesis is that 'You', your joys and your sorrows, your memories and your ambitions, your sense of personal identity and free will, are in fact *no more* [our emphasis] than the behavior of a vast assembly of nerve cells and their associated molecules" (Crick, p.3), he is making a naked assertion with no evidence, no proof, and no argument.

Saying this in not much smarter than saying that "you are what you eat." The scientific words do not make the nonsense easier to swallow. What you are and who you are are distinct from the food you eat or your biochemistry. The geniuses who say such things forget that what you are is your nature, that is, your humanity, and who you are is your distinctive person, signified by your proper name. Reduction to parts is logically dependent on the whole to which the parts belong – in this case the person. The most he can say, but he doesn't say it, is that the behavior of nerve cells and their associated molecules is a *necessary condition* for the occurrence of human persons and their behaviors; or occur when human persons think, feel, decide, and act. It is not, however, a *sufficient condition.* Inquiring minds would like to ask Crick and his fellow materialists: What assembly of neurons is thinking a combination? What assembly of neurons is feeling a combination? What about willing, remembering, a sense of personal identity? This is not to say that the neurons are not firing *when* persons exist and do such things. Is it not, however, the depths of anthropomorphism (i.e., attributing human characteristics to non-human things) to attribute these activities to "*no more* [our emphasis] than the behavior of a vast assembly of nerve cells and their molecules"? In saying things like this, Crick is no longer doing science; he is doing metaphysics, and bad metaphysics at that. This is a good example of what Socrates meant in criticizing those who drifted beyond their competence. Scientists must remind themselves that crackpots are not only found among religious people.

Crick also proposed an "educated" guess as to how life appeared on earth. He calls it directed panspermia. This is the idea that the seeds of life are everywhere present throughout the universe and may have brought living things to earth. This is not an original idea given the fact that the Pre-Socratic philosopher, Anaxagoras, taught a similar idea in the 5th Century B.C., as did St. Augustine in the 5th Century A.D. However, there is a little "scientific" slight of hand here, for the idea of directed panspermia does not explain the origin of those seeds of life.

But if you want to learn about the extent to which the crackpots in science are in circulation, you just have to read through Mary Roach's book: *Spooks: Science Tackles the Afterlife*. Roach is not altogether unsympathetic to experiments by people with scientific credentials and actual scientific accomplishments to weigh, photograph and record the soul. She says in her introduction: "Flawed as it is, science remains the most solid god I've got. And so I decided to see what it had to say on the topic of life after death" (Roach, 12-13). This is her problem, as it is with the others who want scientific, i.e., empirical evidence, for the existence of the soul and the afterlife. While she is properly skeptical about the many episodes and experiments she relates, she still wants to believe that the scientific method is the way to get to the soul. It is in this act of belief that she turns science into religion. Here again, she and the many scientists and scientific quacks she talks about commit the same category mistake that we attributed to Crick; that is, to think of the soul as if it were another body or material thing you could weigh, photograph or record; or to have it discovered or proved by the scientific method.

If that is not enough, we mention, for sheer foolishness the musings of MIT professor, Marvin Minsky, who asks in a quotation from Philip Rieff's *My Life Among the Deathworks* (2006):

> *Should we robotize ourselves and stop dying? I think the answer is clear for the long run because in a few billion years the sun will eventually burn out and everything we've done will go to waste* (Rieff, p. 116).

This guy already has too much time on his hands. He has drained ever ounce of meaning from the word "future." This is the problem when people worry about what is going to happen in a "few billion years" while they can't keep their families together. When you abandon critical common sense, you are left with uncommon nonsense.

CHAPTER FOUR:
Derangements in Religion

Because religion deals with the highest things and the deepest things, the madness in it and of it surpasses the madness of those other human endeavors such as the sciences and the arts. For it is madness in the extreme to practice human sacrifice, infanticide, and cannibalism as religious acts. Such acts are so contrary to nature that the priests who demand them in the name of divinities turn into madness and evil themselves, their societies, and the gods they claim to worship. If the elements of religion consist in a creed (set of beliefs), a code (rules for conduct) and a cult (ways to worship), then such religions which have appeared in history at different times and at different places are the perversion of true religion, which is not only in conformity with nature but transcends it. If there is no transcendence, then religion is little more than an instrument of political control (which in itself is not a bad thing), but it is not religion. The contemporary smugness toward transcendence is traceable to post enlightenment fascination with "the perfectibility of man" as a form of secular redemption. Good and evil (God and Satan) are incorrectly understood as equal and opposite. This is incorrect because "the good" is the standard by which evil is judged and as a result evil is subordinate to the good. For believers it is not enough to merely avoid evil; they are also called upon to pursue good.

Abraham and Isaac

The biblical story of Abraham's temptation to sacrifice Isaac as a religious act commanded by God illustrates the difference between true and false religion as well as the sway of bad ideas in religion. Whatever the many readings of the Abraham – Isaac story – some good, others dopey – one reading is certain. When the angel of the Lord stopped Abraham from committing the ritual human sacrifice of his son, the Biblical writer clearly distinguished between good and bad religion. Abraham, tempted by the fertility cults that were around him in the land of the Philistines, believed that the Lord commanded him to sacrifice Isaac. The test was the Lord's way of showing Abraham how *not* to worship Him. Religion demands worship and sacrifice but not every kind. And so Abraham finds a ram provided by God, we must assume, to offer a proper sacrifice.

The Sacred Feminine

Religious feminists recommend replacing the patriarchal biblical religion with goddesses and the sacred feminine. Indeed talk about "the sacred feminine" has been renewed lately due to the recent success of the novel by Dan Brown, *The Da Vinci Code (2003)*, which exploited the idea of the sacred feminine as one of its themes. It is the case that the religious feminists wish for a return to the religions of Baal and Astarte, in which the sacred feminine was associated, by the way, with priestesses, ritual prostitution, and human sacrifice. For these were the very religions with which God tested Abraham. They are the "strange gods" hankered after and worshipped by the Biblical Jews as mentioned in the books of *Judges, Samuel, Kings, Jeremiah and Hosea*. The wish for such a return can't be serious. But then given the peculiarities of religious madness, one can't be sure. A book by Donna Steichen entitled *Ungodly Rage* (1991) describes the lurid adventures of Catholic feminist nuns with "the sacred feminine." Ironically, the preoccupation with the "sacred feminine" has remained silent with respect to the Virgin Mary. It is a virtue of traditional organized religion to guard against and keep in check such religious tastes and enthusiasms. In doing so, organized religion restrains religious madness and keeps religion within the bounds of sanity.

The thoughtless say "all religions are the same." They are not! Others say "all religions are different." And, of course, we must celebrate the differences. But they are not completely different either. The Abraham – Isaac story shows that worship, conduct and ritual themselves are the same in all religions. This is to say that all religions have all three but the kind of belief, conduct, and ritual differ. Some kinds are true and good, others false and bad. The criteria are *reason and nature*. It is both contrary to reason and contrary to nature for societies to murder their offspring.

Religio-Psychological Sentimentality

In the chapters on education and the behavioral sciences, we used religion as the prime analogue for ideas that were fanatical and stretched beyond the limits of common sense realism. Our intention was to recognize the seriousness and profundity of authentic religion on the one hand and the misuse of that seriousness and profundity by religious pretenders on the other. In the rest of this chapter, we will evaluate certain religious ideas and practices themselves as untenable, as silly, or as horrors. We have already mentioned ritual human sacrifice as one of these horrors. Now we continue by drawing attention to an example of silliness wrapped in religio-psychological sentimentality. In a calendar published in 1982 entitled the John Powell Calendar, Rev. John Powell, S.J. (Society of Jesus) states as the *spiritual bouquet* for February the following words: "If I am to tell you who I really am, I must tell you about my feelings." The *bouquet* for April says "Fully alive people are sensitively aware of all that is good in themselves." Each of the pages recording the months has a facing page with photographic scenes from nature of the sort which are customarily used to adorn greeting cards. As sidebars for each month, Fr. Powell places five feel-good sentences comparable to those prominently displayed on the facing page superimposed on the natural scene. One of them lets us in on whom he must have been reading at the time he uttered it. "Peak experiences of communication inject a new vitality into relationships…. Peak moments help me to get out of myself." (If only he had!) It seems as if this professor of theology taught at Loyola University in Chicago at the time he wrote these musings and was a much sought after retreat master and a popular television personality. The character of his sayings reveal an ersatz religion filtered through the "wisdom" of Abraham Maslow and the other geniuses of humanistic psychology. Divinity, holiness, faith and religion dissolve in a corrosive bath of mawkish sentimentality. A few more quotations from the calendar should emphasize the colossal silliness of these so called religious sentiments: "The fundamental human need is a true and deep love of self, a genuine and joyful self-acceptance, an authentic self-esteem" (One must assume that there are two forms of self-esteem – one authentic and the other inauthentic); "I must continually tell you who I am and you must continually tell me who you are" (We cannot think of a more boring "conversation."); "To reveal myself openly and honestly takes the rarest kind of courage." (We must wonder what Medal of Honor winners think of that one).

Worth mentioning too is a paragraph from the one page biography at the back of the calendar. It reads:

> *John Powell is a deeply human person. The first impression is not of otherworldly holiness, but of here and now humanness. John is deeply empathetic and astonishingly real. Of course, he is a deeply spiritual and solidly religious person, who draws his enlightenment and strength from God. He knows the heart of God as well as the human heart.*

Saying that he knows the human heart is bad enough. But knowing God's heart? WOW! The thoughts and sentiments of the biographer match those of his subject. Should anyone suggest that we thugs from Brooklyn took these words out of context, we and the other voices from the stoop reply in the memorable words of Casey Stengel: "You could look it up." It is all like that. This batch of silly and banal words trying to pass as spirituality or religious consciousness is beyond parody. Indeed it is self-parody. Grown men and women don't think and talk that way. It is unworthy of even adolescent sensibility. It cannot be sustained, and while it is silly, it is not altogether harmless. It is not the pedagogy for the struggles of ordinary life or for combat with the not-so-lovable human monsters we chance to meet. St. Ignatius Loyola, the founder of the Jesuits, would most likely and most happily join his voice with the voices from the stoop in ridiculing such sentimental quackery as that of Fr. Powell, S.J.

Not to be outdone in religious silliness, the Dominican Order had its own embarrassment in Father Matthew Fox, O.P. (Order of Preachers) whose snake oil is more poisonous than Powell's. He denies, for example, the doctrine of original sin, a doctrine that, if any is empirically verifiable, this one is it. In so doing, he is indifferent towards human imperfectability and has to be equally indifferent to the persistence of human tragedy. In denying the doctrine of original sin, Father Fox transforms human finitude into psychological ills; rejects or, at the very least, evades responsibility for one's actions; undermines repentance and denigrates the sacrifice culminated in the blood of Christ. When asked the question: "What does God do all day?" Father Matthew Fox replies: "Why, She enjoys herself." The titles of two of his books are just as cute as his reply. They are *Whee!, We, Wee, All the Way Home*, and *On Becoming a Musical Mystical Bear*. We're not going to fault clever titles. Sometimes they capture the character of a book. We offer these in the context of other features of Fox's conception of spirituality which he still teaches along with prominent feminist witch Miriam "Starhawk" Simos at the Institute in Culture and Creation Spirituality at Holy Names College in Oakland, California. Starhawk practices the old time religion of the "Great Goddess." Fox not only teaches with Starhawk, he hired her in the interests of diversity, we must suppose.

Anne Roche Muggeridge in *The Desolate City* (1986) sums up Fox's "creation spirituality" as "an exotic blend of American Indian animism, feminism, witchcraft, transformational psychology, and currently fashionable medieval mystics" (Muggeridge, 218). Transformation psychology is Abraham Maslow's

"Peak Experience" as presented through Werner Erhard's "est" encounter charades. Fraudulent psychology meets religious silliness. You'd think that Fox's Catholicism would have given him the vision to see through the nonsense. But by the time the Church got around to admonishing him, Fox was no longer a Catholic. In a full page advertisement in the *New York Times* on December 13, 1988 on the occasion of the superior general of the Dominican Order ordering him to take a sabbatical, Fox gave his "final statement before being silenced" wherein he attacked Pope John Paul II, Cardinal Ratzinger (now Pope Benedict XVI), and the Catholic Church. The Dominican Superior General severed himself and the order from Father Fox's pretences.

Celebrating the winter solstice at the Episcopal Cathedral of St. John the Divine complements the religious silliness of Fathers Powell and Fox. The difference is that it is official silliness having the full approval of the authorities at St. John's. This happy return to paganism (*New York Times*, Styles, 12/19/95, Section 9, p.16) which purports to be a celebration of "light and darkness" (shades of gnosticism!) combining the occult, feminism, Wicca (organized witchcraft), the ancient cult of goddesses, magic, environmentalism, pantheism and, of course, the repudiation of Christmas. The solstice celebrations seem to be an attempt to re-enchant the world disenchanted by secularized science and secularized Christianity. It is the desperate attempt on the part of those who have lost their faith but not the need for some kind of faith, the sillier the better.

The Jonestown Horror Show

Putting aside religious silliness at this point and returning to religious horror and to a desperation born in religious madness, we must recall "the Jonestown Massacre" of 1978 and the U.F.O. related lunacy at Rancho Santa Fe, California in 1997.

On the 18th of November, 1978 over 900 members of a religious group called The People's Temple Full Gospel Church and led by a certain Jim Jones died in a mass murder/suicide. The deaths occurred in a jungle settlement in Guyana, South America. The weapon of choice was a fruit punch mixed with cyanide and tranquilizers thereafter mockingly but pitilessly referred to as the Kool-Aid acid test, i.e., the test for blind religious obedience to a kingfish guru – in this case Jim Jones of Indiana by way of San Francisco, California and Jonestown, Guyana. Some members however, including Jones were shot either in suicide or murder. (*The Religious Movements Homepage Project: Peoples Temple, Jonestown, Spring 1998, modified, 2/5/05.*)

Just before the mass murder/suicide, U.S. Congressman Leo Ryan (D., Calif.) along with three members of the media and one deserting Temple member were executed on orders from Rev. Jones. Ryan had just landed in Guyana to investigate human rights abuses at Jonestown, which turned out to be a left-wing millennianist agricultural commune for which Ryan and other California Democrats had some sympathy. The congregation was interracial, an integrationist ideal (unusual at the time).

The theology of the People's Temple, if one could call it theology, was an incoherent mix of Pentecostalism, Christian Social Gospel, socialism, communism, and, as we said before, millennialism (a toxic spiritual cocktail if ever there was one). Both Pentecostalism and millennialism expected an imminent Second Coming of Christ. Russian was studied at Jonestown and contributions were sent to Moscow as financial support for the Communist government. Jones thought of himself as a reincarnation of Jesus and Lenin. It is no surprise that Jones used promiscuous sex to control members of the congregation. Our contemporary preoccupation with sexual prowess on the part of both males and females, merely confirms the fact that the sins of the flesh have become more deadly. The voices from the stoop remind us of original sin and that there are sins which are not so original.

Guyana, a multi-racial country and the only English-speaking nation in South America, was a socialist republic. Its black minority government was pleased to be the host and a refuge for North Americans fleeing a racist and oppressive capitalist regime. One problem was, however, that Jones, a champion of an integrated interracial commune was responsible, as someone said at the time of the massacre, for killing more blacks in one day than the Ku Klux Klan had in its entire history.

Clichés passing themselves off as explanatory theories of the massacre abounded. One of them was that Jonestown was a CIA plot in mind control experiments. Another was a supposed fear of retribution by the government of the United States for the commune's pro-Communist and anti-American posture. Psychological explanations based on assumptions of brainwashing and the blind obedience associated with religion itself did not satisfactorily account for what happened and why. Just as the U.S. State Department secularists could not understand the importance of religion at the time of the Iranian revolution in 1979, so too attempts at explaining the Jonestown Massacre without addressing religious ideas — bad religious ideas — were futile. The bad idea of millennialism combined with heady revolutionary politics along with a concept of revolutionary suicide, i.e., killing oneself in order to bring about the socialist revolution or the Second Coming of Christ and His thousand year reign — whichever might be the preferred event. Sounds nuts? It is! But these are among the perennially bad ideas to which religion is subject. The Jonestown affair was a violation of true religion because it was a violation of nature and reason.

The Rancho Santa Fe Lunacy

What happened at Jonestown inspires pity for the members of the congregation. The same cannot be said about the members of the Rancho Santa Fe episode. The pity must be reserved for the extent to which that bad mix of religious horror and religious foolishness can reach. Heaven's Gate was the name of a community founded near San Diego by Marshall Applewhite and Bonnie Nettles, two lunatics if there ever were such. Nettles was already dead when

Applewhite gently persuaded 39 members of the community to take their own lives or to have them taken if they did not do so willingly on the occasion of the appearance of the Hale-Bopp comet purportedly accompanied by a UFO (Unidentified Flying Object) that would take them to "Heaven," but apparently only if they were dead (*The Religious Movements Homepage Project: Heaven's Gate, 2005. See also Herman de Tollenaere, Indian Skeptic, August 15, 1997*).

In a parody of the Christian monastic vows of poverty, chastity, and obedience, the members gave up their personal possessions, earning a communal living by providing their services as professional web designers; some were castrated, and their obedience was displayed in doing what Applewhite told them to do. There was no chance that these folks could integrate traditional Christian practice with a show-biz theology of sci-fi junk dumped on the public by the media geniuses. Hey, it sells! Applewhite's religion, combined with the perennial junk theology of Gnosticism and Manicheanism, was too tempting a religious dish to resist. Their ritual suicide carried out in shifts was achieved by drinking a "potion" of phenobarbital, vodka and apple juice. A video tape made by the last to die showed the bodies in bunk beds, displayed in purple blankets and wearing identical Nike sneakers – a macabre enactment of the commercial slogan "Dressed for success." The video was shown by the media in their coverage of the suicides to the cacophony of the psycho- and socio-babblers. The members had also packed suitcases and money for the trip on the spaceship, i.e., the UFO. Life on earth was evil, saturated as it was by "Luciferians." Gnosticism and Manicheanism is never far from stuff like this.

A little more of its history is important to mention here so as to understand better the Heaven's Gate phenomenon. Sometime in the 1970s, Applewhite, a music teacher, was a patient in an insane, oops – sorry, psychiatric asylum where Bonnie Nettles was his nurse. She was a member of the Theosophical Society in Houston, Texas and wrote the astrology column for a local newspaper. Nettles and Applewhite read together a book called *The Secret Doctrine* (shades of Gnosticism again!) written by Madame Blavatsky, the Russian founder of a religio-philosophical movement called Theosophy. She claimed to have spent seven years in Tibet when and where she became initiated into the mysteries of the occult. Like Lamont (The Shadow) Cranston she learned the power "to cloud men's minds." Unlike Cranston who used that power to fight "the evil that lurks in the hearts of men," Madame Blavatsky used it to propagate bad religious ideas, which culminated in the events at Rancho Santa Fe. Later, Blavatsky went to India for another dose of eastern religious doctrine. The title of her most famous work is *Isis Unveiled (1877)*. This book adds the ingredient of the Egyptian goddess to her *pasticcio* of religious sensibility.

Theosophy and the Eastern Temptation

Anne "Sophie" Besant, an English atheist and a member of the socialist Fabian Society, left her Protestant clergyman husband to become a disciple and the biographer of Madame Blavatsky, through whom she was introduced to the mysteries of the exotic east. In 1907 she became the president of the Theosophical Society. Besant established a headquarters in California and set up around 1927 her protégé, Jiddu Krishnamurti, as the one she proclaimed the new Messiah – "the vehicle of the World Teacher." To his credit, Krishnamurti resigned his position as Messiah (Can you resign as Messiah?) in 1929 declaring that he did not believe that California was the cradle of the "new race" as predicted by Madame Blavatsky. Applewhite and Nettles, however, went to California to be in the religious environment created by Blavatsky and Besant. They just added their own up-to-date imaginative touches to that environment. At Rancho Santa Fe the dialectic of religious silliness and religious horror was played out in such a way as if to exclaim: "This is the logic of bad religious ideas!" The silliness, however, was not sufficiently muted by the horror of mass suicide, such that one could feel the same degree of pity that one feels about the residents of Jonestown.

The more recent importation of Indian or Indian-type gurus into the religious consciousness of some Westerners is worth mentioning as "another fine mess" (apologies to Laurel and Hardy) of religious silliness. Although the directory of such gurus is large, we need only attend to a few to make the point. The first is the Maharishi Mahesh Yogi, who set up shop in Los Angeles during the '60s but returned to India only to be discovered in his Ashram by the most famous Rock group in the world: The Beatles. If, as John Lennon said, the Beatles were "bigger than Jesus," then their guru had to be "bigger than Jesus." Thus transcendental meditation (TM), the Maharishi's technique for getting beyond oneself and united with the whole cosmos, replaced the "Our Father" and the "Act of Contrition" for devotees of the Beatles and their gurus. But to no serious person's surprise, the Maharishi and Transcendental Meditation passed into the museum of religious follies. Jesus, however, is bigger than ever.

Then there is the Swami Satchidananda who also achieved fame through his association with Rock music, indeed at the quintessential Rock Festival of all time: Woodstock (1969). Sitting on a white bedspread, engulfed by speakers, microphones and around 500,000 new agers engaged in a religious frenzy of sex, drugs, and rock and roll, the Swami blended his words and blessings to the sounds of Jimi Hendrix, Janis Joplin, the Who, the Grateful Dead and others of the species of Rock. The Swami could have been a contender for the Maharishi's crown of Guru of all gurus (of the time), but he settled in 1973 for a one way ticket to the Satchidananda Ashram–Yogaville in Connecticut. Regrettably, a nice smart girl from Brooklyn, Carole King (songwriter and singer), was one of his groupies. And has anyone else noticed that the behavior of rock concert audiences looks like, although does not sound like the behavior of the participants of the Arab Street?

As for our Indian-type guru, we have Richard Alpert, a.k.a, Baba Ram Das, who described himself as "the water-boy of the team" (of gurus that is), "a Western Jewish boy from Boston who studied Hinduism." He was more than that. He was a Harvard psychology professor who along with his colleague,

Timothy Leary, of "tune in, turn on, drop out" fame, had enormous influence on the devotees of that form of new age religion which combined humanistic psychology, drugs (especially LSD), and Indian mysticism. Nor should we forget that the new age religion had strong diplomatic relations with the shrine of unlimited pan-sexualism, Esalen Institute at Big Sur, California. Alpert wrote a book too! *Be Here Now*, the psycho-religious handbook for the New Age initiates. This stuff was bad religion, bad psychology and bad medicine, but it too has had its day.

This lust for the exotic religions of the East is understandable because of natural restlessness and the natural desire for novelty. Hinduism and Buddhism do offer techniques of meditation and self-control such as Yoga and Zen. Such techniques are also understandable given the natural desire and restlessness for God, but neither Buddhism nor Hinduism satisfies the desire for a personal God who is the proper object for contemplation. Popular Hinduism is polytheistic (a doctrine incompatible with the Divine Nature) while theological Hinduism is pantheistic and holds at the same time that the world is an illusion (Maya). In denying a personal God, Buddhism can be correctly described as "atheistic." In such a religion, hope, if there can be such a thing, is a resignation before nothingness. A religion devoid of hope is contrary to human desire and to human reason.

Just as there are those who look for love in all the wrong places, so too there are those who look for God in all the wrong places. If wanderlusting Westerners can learn some wisdom from fiction, even a minor fiction, then they will say along with Dorothy in *The Wizard of Oz*: "There's no place like home."

Theology of "Liberation"

For religious silliness connected to politics, we have the canonization of Che Guevara, Marxist revolutionary and romanticized killer, by an ex-Maryknoll priest with the words "Santo Che." As Jesus was supposed to have left an imprint of his face on Veronica's veil when she wiped his face with it on the way to Calvary, so too we have the face of Santo Che imprinted on tee-shirts and sold all over the world. A recent movie, "*Motorcycle Diaries* (2004)," and a new play by the movie's screenwriter, José Rivera, are recent and current testimonials to the perpetual veneration of "Santo Che." At any rate, politicized distortions of history when sanctified by religious nomenclature do have their rhetorical effect.

This is true in the case of Latin American Liberation Theology, or as its cheerleaders instruct us to call it, the theology of liberation. For this theology "Jesu Cristo Liberador" (Jesus Christ, Liberator) is the rhetorical key to reading the gospel in terms of Marxist revolutionary politics, anti-capitalism and class warfare. And although Pope John Paul II censured theologians Gustavo Gutierrez, O.P.(*A Theology of Liberation, 1973*) Leonardo Boff, O.F.M. (*Jesus Christ Liberator: A Critical Christology for Our Time, 1978*) and Jon Sobrino, S.J. (*The True Church and the Poor, 1984*), three prominent theologians of liberation, he also lent rhetorical support to the movement by approvingly employing a phrase on December 2, 1989 dear to the theology of liberation and the class warfare it endorses, namely, "the preferential option for the poor." We have to believe that John Paul II used the expression in the traditional Christian sense of detachment from wealth and the use of it not only to care for the poor but to create a civilization of the specifically human things as science, art, morality and law – a civilization wealthy enough to care for the poor such that they too can participate in those human things. We have to believe also that he did not use it in the sense that poverty is a virtue in itself and wealth a vice so that an elite class of messiahs would forcefully and socialistically redistribute wealth in order to exercise that "preferential option for the poor." It seems that this was the interpretation given to the expression by the Latin American theologians of liberation masked by the Biblical (Old and New Testaments) rhetoric of "social justice," a code expression for economic justice (a fine old Marxist idea). The conferences of Latin American bishops at Medellin, (coincidentally the site of the Columbian drug cartel) Columbia (1968) and Pueblo, Mexico (1979) had already used the expression approvingly. The desire to be with "los pobres de la tierra" requires ready satisfaction. "Quantanamera!"

Cuckoo Ecumenism

Another lapse of prudence on the part of John Paul II, albeit born of his holiness, kindness and respect for "the other," was his kissing of the *Koran* at the Vatican on May 14, 1999 during a meeting with Muslim representatives. As a colleague of ours said at the time: "Once an actor, always an actor." Apparently, the saintly Pope forgot, or chose to forget, in a so-called ecumenical moment, Islam's posture toward Christianity? Joe Ecclesia [pseudonym] would have reminded him and other bishops inclined toward a schmaltzy ecumenism with the following admonition:

> *You bishops might ... teach us the history of Islam. We are aware of the bloodthirsty Christian Crusaders – much of that information is false and one-sided, but we'll let that go – but how many of your flock know even the most basic facts about Islam's savage attacks on Christianity: How many Catholics know that Muhammad [this student of a Arian priest] planned more than 50 military campaigns, mostly against Arabs, and personally led some 20 of them? [Doesn't sound much like "Teach all nations"] How many know that North Africa, the Middle East, and Turkey were once Christian, but fell prey to Muslim invasions: How many have heard of Tours, of the sack and burning of Monte Cassino, of the hundreds of thousands of Christians enslaved [and continue to be enslaved] by Muslims over the last 1400 years? How many of your flock could tell you anything at all about the Reconquista in Spain, the*

siege of Constantinople, the battle of Lepanto? Ignorance may be
bliss, Your Excellenc[ies], but it can also be a sword in the heart (Joe
Ecclesia, "The I – Word," Chronicles, August 2006, p,42).

And how can one have respect for current Muslim terrorists setting up headquarters in hospitals, and using women and children as shields or in being suicide bombers, all in the name of Islam? What must they themselves in moments of rational reflection or others think of their dignity and self-respect when they negotiate prisoner exchanges in such ratios as 600 of theirs to two of their enemies? They must console themselves after such reflection that they made a good deal at the bazaar – that they are shrewd and cunning traders.

But what of Allah in all this? To attribute such acts of ignobility and dishonor to His will is blasphemy, if nature and reason count for something. But then Muslims are fatalists. And as such they must attribute everything that happens to God's will and nothing to human agency. Islamic political theology, which is theocratic, complements its metaphysical fatalism by justifying the union of the divine will of Allah and the human will of the mullahs.

The bad religious ideas connected to politics rest on the confusion between the desire and restlessness to be with God and the desire to be God or the Messiah. It is analogous to the desire to be God in pantheistic New Age religion. If you are already God, there is no point to being with God or God being with you.

CHAPTER FIVE:
Lunacy in the Law

Law versus Lawyers

What is it about the rule of law that so offends lawyers that they are prepared to corrupt it? And why do lawyers lie? The answer is simple enough. We can state it right at the beginning of our considerations about law's lunacy. The law and, *a fortiori*, the rule of law places limits on what they want to say and do as regards power, prestige and money. Because lawyers study law, they become more familiar with it than do ordinary citizens. That familiarity, as the maxim warns, breeds contempt.

Because religion deals with the highest things or deepest things, indeed divine things, its corruption and madness is comparable to its height and depth, as we said in the last chapter. The horror is most horrible in the case of sacrificial murder and for the sake of cannibalism while the foolishness is most foolish in its sentimentality as expressed, for example, in the popular Beatles song: "All You Need is Love."

Law and Civilization

The law, however, is not specifically about divine things but about human things. We must note that for prevailing premodern thought the human things were distinct but not separate from the divine things. For prevailing modern thought, however, from Machiavelli on, human things are separate, or ideally proposed as separate, from divine things as exemplified in Thomas Jefferson's famous expression of "a wall of separation" between Church and State. And in republics, direct or representative, the law rules and is sovereign. Republics are the best kind of regime, in that they permit the exercise of liberty and the growth of civilization. We are not talking about culture. Every society has a culture. Not every society is a civilization. For one of the marks of a civilization is the rule of law. And not every society is ruled by law. Human beings flourish and are most human when they govern themselves. That is to say when ruling and being ruled by law. Under these conditions the other features of civilization emerge, namely, economic prosperity, art, science, and philosophy.

In the context of republics, the profession of law is noble. It is for this reason that the rule of lawyers is ignoble and a corruption of law. This is not to say that there are not noble lawyers. Thomas More comes immediately to mind as does Robert Bork who more recently (1987) tried patiently and honorably to teach his antagonistic inquisitors on the Senate Judiciary Committee about law, the U.S. Constitution, and interpreting that Constitution. Those antagonists were lawyers themselves who were committed to destroying his nomination to the Supreme Court. The contrast between their behavior and his at the hearings was remarkable, his was to be a teacher of the law; theirs was to play "gotcha." Thomas More was executed by Henry VIII for his defense of the rule of law; Bork's career and reputation as a judge were besmirched for his.

Having acknowledged the obvious fact that not all lawyers are corrupters of the law and, indeed, some are noble and honorable men as their profession would require them to be, we must also acknowledge that for both ordinary and extraordinary people, the honesty and integrity of lawyers is suspect. Because of their familiarity with one of the best things in human life — the rule of law — their acts of corruption tend toward the worse. As the voices from the stoop say, "*Corruptio optimi, pessima*" (The corruption of the best is the worst).

Plato, Jesus, and Shakespeare on Lawyers

As far as the testimony of extraordinary people, we shall mention three: Plato, Jesus, and Shakespeare. People don't get more extraordinary than they. In the dialogue *Apology*, Socrates' prosecuting attorney, Meletus, is described as a bully (26e) who lies (34b) and who does not *care* about the law and justice (24c, 26 a & b). But in the dialogue *Theaetetus* Plato is not just criticizing one lawyer who is prosecuting his teacher and friend; he is speaking about lawyers more generally. The dialogue says:

> [I speak of] the profession of those paragons of intellect known as
> orators and lawyers. There you have men, who use their skill to
> produce conviction, not by instruction, but by making people believe
> whatever they want them to believe. You can hardly imagine teach-
> ers so clever as to be able, in the short time allowed by the clock, to
> instruct their hearers thoroughly in the true facts of a case of rob-
> bery or other violence which those hearers had not witnessed (201b
> Cornford translation).

It is the tendency toward sophistry (making people believe whatever they want them to believe) that lawyers find irresistible in the attempt to win a case rather than to see justice done. Furthermore, Plato speaks of sophistry used to convict. Recent events have demonstrated that lawyers will attempt to produce acquittal for clients they know to be guilty, forgetting or ignoring, per-haps, that they have responsibilities as officers of the court and not only as rep-resentatives of their clients. This happens when lawyers believe that there are no such things as justice and injustice, only the process and strategies employed in litigation within an adversary system. This belief abandons the substance of justice for the process of litigation. It also happens when lawyers believe that there are oppressed categories of persons who cannot, because of their oppres-sion, be guilty of any crime. A corollary of this belief is that the system, usually the capitalist system, is regarded as the cause or perpetrator of either criminal or civil illegality. Such bad ideas, merged with the sophistry, are part of the lunacy in the theory and practice of law during the recent history of the West.

Jesus' comments are even harsher than Plato's. In Luke's gospel, he says:

> *Woe to you lawyers also [he has just pronounced woes on the Phari-*
> *sees] because you load men with oppressive burdens and you your-*
> *selves with one of you fingers do not touch the burdens. Woe to you!*
> *For you build the tombs of the prophets whereas your fathers killed*
> *them. So then you are witnesses and approve of the deeds of your fa-*
> *thers; for they indeed killed them and you build their tombs...Woe*
> *to you lawyers because you have taken away the key to knowledge,*
> *you have not entered yourselves and those who were entering you*
> *have hindered (Luke, 11,46-49; 52).*

No need for fancy exegesis here.

Shakespeare's comments complement neatly those of Plato and Jesus. The most famous, albeit controversial, expresses what many ordinary people, in their frustration with legalistic sophisms, would like to say and not only in their hearts. "The first thing we do is let's kill all the lawyers" (*Henry VI*, Part 2, Act 4, Scene 2). The line is controversial because some lawyers (the law firm of Dickstein, Shapiro, Morin and Oshinsky) have argued that the line is really meant to be in praise of lawyers, that is to say, that it is ironic. Since the line is uttered, they say, by a plotter of treachery, it is intended to eliminate the defenders of society and the guardians of independent thinking. The context of the play, however, reveals the sophistry of this bit of self-defense on the part of lawyers. Henry VI was a corrupt tyrant who controlled the administration of justice by means of his lawyers. Our critical common sense realism tempts us to say that although some lawyers should be killed, not all lawyers should be; for a society with honest lawyers is better than one with no lawyers.

In the churchyard scene in *Hamlet*, there are words about lawyers describing their activities such that they resonated with Shakespeare's Elizabethan audience and no doubt resonate with current audiences. Hamlet, in comic relief, speaks as the clowns dig in the graveyard:

There's another [skull]: why may not that be the skull of a lawyer?
Where be his quiddities now, his quillets, his cases, his tenures and
his tricks? Why does he suffer this rude knave now to knock him
about the sconce with a dirty shovel and will not tell him of his ac-
tion of battery? Hum! This fellow might be in's time a great buyer of
land, with his statutes, his recognizances, his fines, his double vouch-
ers, his recoveries: is this the fine of his fines, and the recovery of his
recoveries, to have his fine pate full of fine dirt? Will his vouchers
vouch him no more of his purchases, and double ones too, than the
length and breadth of a pair of indentures? The very conveyance of
his lands will hardly lie in this box, and must the inheritor himself
have no more, ha? (Act V, Scene I).

Law and Justice

It would be a serious understatement to say that the voices from the
stoop are pleased to find themselves in such excellent company as that of Plato,
Jesus, and Shakespeare on the issue of lawyers manipulating the law. But they
and the voices speak mainly, if not completely, about lawyers and the practice
of law. The bad ideas, whether they influence directly or not the practice of
law, are in the theory of law. They do, however, influence the teaching of law
in law schools, in courses on jurisprudence but also in courses on criminal and
civil law. In an earlier chapter we alluded to a theory of law that espouses and
propounds the preposterous notion that justice is entirely separate from the
concept of law. This silliness and disregard for common sense is done in the
face of the statue of Lady Justice with her blindfold and her scale. It does take
gall and arrogance to flout this historical symbol which is found throughout
the transhistorical archaeology of the world of law. The time worn expression
"the scales of justice" must be regarded with professional contempt by such
theorists.

Let's look at an example from a highly regarded text in the philosophy of law — highly regarded by those who wrap themselves in the cloak of Modernity and think that they are expounding a "scientific" concept of law.

Hans Kelsen, in his representative book professing the positivist theory of law (what "positivist" means here will be evident from the words we quote), says without a hint of irony:

> As used in these investigations, the concept of law has no moral connotation whatsoever. It designates a specific technique of social organization. The problem of law, as a scientific problem, is the problem of social technique, not a problem of morals. The statement "A certain social order has the character of law, is a legal order," does not imply the moral judgment that this order is good or just. There are legal orders which are from a certain point of view, [sic] unjust. Law and justice are two different concepts. Law as distinguished from justice is positive law. It is the concept of positive law which is here in question; and a science of positive law must be clearly distinguished from a philosophy of justice (General Theory of Law and State, 1945, p. 5).

The lack of understanding of both the concept of law and the concept of justice takes the breath away from ordinary intelligent people as, for example, those who hang out on the stoops. Take, for example, the statement Kelsen calls a designation of law, i.e., a definition without any moral connotation. (For our purposes here, we are not distinguishing positivism from logical positivism.) The concept of law "designates a specific technique of law." Aside from the circularity of the statement, we must ask about what "specific technique"? He does not say here or elsewhere in the book what that specific technique is. He cannot do so because he has so dogmatically separated the concept of law from the concept of justice. The concepts of law and justice are indeed distinct, but, as we argued in our discussion of the fact/value distinction, they are not two separate modes of discourse that have nothing to do with each other. Here is the way Kelsen puts the dogma of the fact-value divorce:

> *But which human needs are worthy of being satisfied and especially what is their proper order of rank? These questions cannot be answered by rational cognition. The decision of these questions is a judgment of value, determined by emotional factors, and is, therefore, subjective in character, valid only for the judging subject therefore, relative only (Kelsen, p.6).*

He has it all here: the dogma and all its parts. Judgments of value are non-cognitive; they are emotive; they are subjective and they are relative. One would think that values such as knowledge, health, wealth, power, beauty, pleasure and happiness are not subjective or relative at all. They are objective and universal. They are values that everyone wants and pursues. They are things wanted and pursued because they are recognized and understood as things to be desired and possessed. The emotion and desire follow upon the recognition. The order of preference may vary but the variation is within an objective context. If we wanted to be picky, and we do with bad ideas, we would say the phrase "judgment of value" is not emotive at all. Emotions do not make judgments; cognition does.

Let us say that the connection between law and justice is found in the understanding of law as rational (i.e., cognitive) and authoritative public commands to establish justice. And justice means that everyone gets what he or she deserves, whether it be reward or punishment. That is what the "specific technique" of social organization called law *is*. Separated from justice the technique is not specific at all and can refer to any kind of organization that the powerful in any society can dictate. To say that laws do not achieve perfect justice is not wisdom but foolishness. No human institutions are infallible – as if again we had to say so. But we do have to say so with guys like Kelsen because he believes his philosophical adversaries require perfect justice for the law.

Consider what he says in the following:

> *To free the concept of law from the idea of justice is difficult because both are constantly confused in non-scientific political thought as well as in general speech, and because this confusion corresponds to the individual tendency to make positive law appear as just* (Kelsen, p. 5).

Freeing the concept of law from the idea of justice is not difficult because they are confused in general speech and in non-scientific political thought; it is difficult because they have not been and cannot be separated in general speech or in "non-scientific" political thought. The concepts are distinct but related, as we have already said. Thinking about one entails thinking about whether the law or a law is called just or unjust. It is Kelsen who has the ideological bias when he rejects general speech (i.e., common sense) and non-scientific political thought (Aristotle, Plato, Cicero, Aquinas and Hooker) in favor of what he thinks is scientific thought, namely the dogmatic separation of fact from value and, we must suppose, the "method" of empirical verification.

In the first place empirical verification is not a special method. It is looking, hearing, smelling, touching, tasting and understanding what is being perceived. With respect to law, we look, hear and understand that the concept of law is always related either to justice or injustice (except in some law schools). This is not positivism, of course, which cannot distinguish meaning from truth, confusing them as it does with "the verificationist principle of meaning" which is the characteristic doctrine of positivism. But it is critical common sense realism and it is true. Separating the concepts of law and justice is neither scientific nor true. To say that the concept of law, as in the laws of physics, is not related to justice commits two fallacies in logic: the fallacy of equivocation, i.e., confusing two different meanings of law in the same discussion and the fallacy of *ignoratio elenchi*, as they say on the stoop, i.e., the fallacy of irrelevancy.

Further evidence that Kelsen and the positivists do not know what they are talking about shows up when they confuse the concept of justice with that of happiness:

> *What does it really mean to say that a social order is a just one? It means that this order regulates the behavior of men in a way satisfactory to all men, that is to say, so that all men find their happiness in it. The longing for justice is men's [sic] eternal longing for happiness. It is happiness that man cannot find as an isolated individual and hence seeks in society. Justice is social happiness (Kelsen, p. 6).*

To say that a social order is just is *not* to say that "all men find their happiness in it." Kelsen is putting words in the mouths of his adversaries. A social order is just when the citizens get what they deserve as regards reward and punishment, rights and duties, and are publicly perceived to get what they deserve. Justice is *not* social happiness but rather aims at social happiness. Social happiness is the satisfaction of the citizens in the law performing excellently and in their performing excellently. For that satisfaction neither their own performance nor that of the law has to be perfect; their performances do have to be good.

Another mistake Kelsen and his fellow positivists make is on the relation of God's will to law in natural law doctrine. The relevance of this issue is whether law as such is primarily an expression of reason or of will:

> *The will of God is — in the natural law doctrine — identical with nature in so far as nature is conceived of as created by God, and the laws of nature as expression of God's will (Kelsen, p. 8).*

This is precisely what natural law doctrine is not. Natural law doctrine holds that there are universal principles of right and wrong accessible to human beings consistent with their rational nature and end, and by which they can formulate positive law to govern themselves. C.S. Lewis calls it the Tao. Rather, in natural law doctrine, the laws of nature (both physical and moral) are the expression of God's reason –– his intelligence and executed by His will. In natural law doctrine, law is an expression of reason or it is not law.

Definitions of Law: Fictional and Actual

Logical Positivists were not the first "thinkers" to separate the concept of law from that of justice and to define law as the will of the ruler or rulers. The Sophists did so in the Pre-modern world. The best known example is that of Thrasymachus, a character in Plato's *Republic* who in effect denies that justice is real when he says that "justice is the advantage of the stronger" (*Republic*, 341a), an idea more popularly rendered in a less nuanced way as "might makes right." "Justice" is an empty word used in the rhetoric of the powerful to deceive their subjects into believing that the ruler's injustice is really justice.

The modern versions of this idea, however, lack the cynicism that Plato attaches to Thrasymachus' so called realistic definition of justice. A philosopher such as Thomas Hobbes understands justice as the will and power of the ruler, however incomplete it may be, to thwart, among other motives, subversion of the rule of law by appeals to conscience by those who would set individual conscience against the law. For Hobbes the law is the public conscience. On this point he is quite right. Civil disobedience is not to be countenanced, for it is a mark of the return of "the war of every man against every man" (*Leviathan*, 1651, Pt 1, Chap.13).

A philosopher of law, who follows Hobbes in restricting the definition of law to the will and command of rulers, is John Austin. In his *Lectures on Jurisprudence* (1832), he gives a utilitarian twist to law. From Austin, therefore, and from other utilitarians we learn the "profound truth" that law and morality are useful. Imagine that! But what about the not so profound idea that the concept of law itself means social utility which then John Stuart Mill, utilitarian extraordinaire, who, because he interprets the term utility as pleasure, must *a fortiori* take the law to mean social pleasure. It is quite a different matter to say that law *is* useful from saying the law *means* useful.

Austin's definition, aside from its association with utilitarianism, simply put, is that law is the command of the sovereign (*Lectures on Jurisprudence, Lecture I*). A command, he says, is "a signification of desire" on the part of "political superiors to political inferiors." While he does say that law is "a rule laid down for the guidance of an intelligent being by an intelligent being having power over him," the notion of intelligence or reason is overshadowed by that of desire, will, and force in this definition. But in saying that "the command of the lawgiver" is law, Austin makes a distinction between the legislator and the judge – a distinction lost in the definition of law given by Oliver Wendell Holmes, Jr. Austin says that "the lawgiver commands that thieves be hanged. A specific theft and a specified thief being given, the judge commands the thief shall be hanged, agreeably to the command of the lawgiver" (*Lectures on Jurisprudence, Lecture I*).

Supreme Court Justice Holmes, a so-called legal realist, spoils his actual common sense activity as a judge with his bad theory of law. Not only that, he confuses the parts that legislators and judges have in the execution of law. He asserts "The prophecies of what the courts will do in fact, and *nothing more pretentious* [our emphasis] are what I mean by the law" ("The Path of the Law," 10 *Harvard Law Review* 457 [1897]). In other words, the words of the law do not mean what they say but what the judges say they mean, something we can call Alice in Wonderland Jurisprudence.

This is realism? In what sense can a concept of law as prediction be called realistic? Are we to accept that "weather" is what the weathermen say it is? If defenders of this concept of law want to call it something, then let them call it pragmatism, not realism. What Holmes says elsewhere in his essay *is* realistic. "The law is the witness and external deposit of our moral life. Its history is the history of the moral development of the race. The practice of it, in spite of popular jests, tends to make good citizens and good men" ("The Path of the Law"). And we add to this realistic conception that the educative character of the law is by means of the authority of political society.

Then we have more bad ideas in the thinking of Holmes when in a few paragraphs later in the same essay he states the following contradictory assertion:

> I hope that my illustrations have shown the danger, both to speculation and to practice of confounding morality with law [!] and the trap that legal language lays for us on that side of our way. For my own part, I often doubt whether it would not be a gain if every word of moral significance could be banished from the law altogether, and other words adopted which should convey legal ideas uncolored by anything outside the law.

Welcome to Wonderland, Alice!

Bad Ideas and Bad Decisions

The only way we can hope to unravel this paradox in Holmes' thought is to say that he has not distinguished clearly enough for himself the nature of law from the process of law. What he seems to want to do is to separate moral doctrines and partisan policy preferences from legal procedure. This is indeed a good intention, which did go awry, however, in the late 20th and early 21st centuries with such unconstitutional decisions of the monarchical judiciary against the right to life as *Roe* (1973) and against the right to private property as *Kelo* (2005). But rationally unrestrained judge-made law is unavoidable when you have definitions of law such as that of Holmes and even sound systems as that of British Common Law and the principle of *stare decisis*. What seems to count as legal realism, then, is that while legislators are ideally thought to be lawmakers, what is really the case is that judges make law.

It is no pleasure to criticize men such as Holmes in comparison with those like "Orgone box," Wilhelm Reich, and sex expert, Alfred Kinsey, who deserve not only criticism but contempt. For Holmes was a thrice-wounded Civil War hero whose practical judgments were wiser than his theoretical judgments. Such actions do not go forgotten in the course of our criticism. We must say, however, that even his practical judgments are sometimes of dubious wisdom, as in the *Buck v. Bell* decision of 1927 wherein Holmes put himself into the company of such social Darwinists as Francis Galton who gave us the term "eugenics," Herbert Spencer, of "survival of the fittest" fame and Margaret Sanger, the grand-dame of Social Darwinism as well as the founder of the Planned Parenthood Organization — purveyor of condoms for children, proponent of abortion on demand, as well as of euthanasia and sterilization of the unfit.

Easily forgotten by the enlightened Social Darwinists is the capture, sale and display of Ota Benga, an African pygmy showcased at the St. Louis World's Fair in 1904. Darwinism demands the existence of intermediate species. This "living display" of the stages of evolution failed to recognize that Ota Benga was a human being. After the Fair, Social Darwinists were unconcerned that he was transferred from the Museum of Natural History in New York and then locked in the monkey house at the Bronx Zoo. *The New York Times* reported that "the joint man-and-monkey exhibition was the most interesting in Bronx Park." This treatment of Ota Benga was not without controversy — a matter to be resolved by history. Tragically, Ota Benga's life ended in suicide in 1916. However, Darwinism, Social Darwinism and scientism continue (Cynthia Crossen, "How Pygmy Ota Benga Ended up in Bronx Zoo as Darwinism Dawned," *Wall Street Journal*, 2/6/06, p. B1).

Oliver Wendell Holmes, Jr. was a member of what Pope John Paul II called "the culture of death" gang whose membership included such Nazi euthanasia practitioners as Dr. Christian Wirth. Holmes was not shy in declaring that there are lives "unworthy of life." Exterminations are what happen when introduced by such "scientific' ideas as "pure gene pools." We are in the death-dance of a decadent democracy choreographed by thoughtless scientists and the careless lawyers.

The high-sounding nonsense passing for wisdom from Supreme Court Justice Anthony Kennedy in the *Planned Parenthood v. Casey* decision of 1992 serves as the epigram for the notion of freedom among the cultural elite. Kennedy wrote: "At the heart of liberty, is the right to define one's own concept of existence, of meaning, of the universe and of the mystery of life." Since when did the concepts of existence, meaning, the universe, and the mystery of life become private concepts of the anomic-autonomic individual? They have become so since the cultured despisers of civilization, to paraphrase Edmund Burke in his *Letter to a Noble Lord*, pursued a liberty separable from order, from virtue, from morals, and from religion. They brought it about that liberty, in itself one of the first blessings, should in its perversion become the greatest curse which could fall on mankind. Before and after Friedrich Nietzsche announced, not without some regret, that God is Dead (*The Joyful Wisdom*, 1882), God had already been "killed" by the sophistry of foolish philosophers, foolish lawyers, foolish scientists and foolish artists committed to the death of Western Civilization.

In the *Buck v. Bell* case, a young woman, Carrie Buck, was described as a promiscuous mental defective who for the public interest should be sterilized. In this notorious case, Holmes delivered himself of the following unsterilized opinion:

> It is better for all the world if instead of waiting to execute degenerate offspring for crimes or to let them starve for their imbecility, society can prevent those who are manifestly unfit for continuing their kind. The principle that sustains compulsory vaccination is broad

enough to cover cutting the fallopian tubes [Really, Justice Holmes!].
Three generations of imbeciles are enough.

As that great wise detective from the East, Charlie Chan, says: "If man places self in way of suspicion, must not be surprised if he receive poke in the eye."

The Carrie Buck story did not end with the decision. As it turned out, Carrie Buck's daughter, Vivian, was not feebleminded. Her report card on completion of the first grade showed that she was a "B" student, received an "A" in conduct and was on the honor roll (Paul Lombardo, "Eugenic Sterilization Laws," *Image Archive on the American Eugenics Movement*, Cold Spring Harbor Laboratory, 2006).

Bad ideas feed on other bad ideas. Bad theoretical ideas usually (not necessarily) produce bad practical decisions. Holmes' bad theoretical idea of the definition of law was complemented by his bad decision and supporting opinion in *Buck v. Bell*. Eugenicists privately supported such practices as euthanasia and even genocide, but it was laws regarding sterilization that received support from the American eugenics movement of which Holmes was a member.

The movement was promoted by an American clergy preaching the gospel of progress. The Americans got their inspiration from Francis Galton, Charles Darwin's cousin, who aimed at improving the human species by advocating the "fit" to breed more and the "unfit" to breed less or not at all. Good old psychologist and Freud's American agent, G. Stanley Hall, held that the Bible should be interpreted as a book on eugenics. He even published a biography of Jesus as the eugenic "superman." Such are the brainstorms of someone who studied his theology at Union Theological Seminary. This stuff is beyond parody.

By 1914 liberal Protestant churches and Reform synagogues sponsored sermons on the subject of eugenics. There were even two, not altogether cooperative, Catholic priests on a committee devoted to eugenic doctrine. They resigned after Pope Pius XI condemned sterilization in 1930. By then the eugenics movement was joined with that of the birth control movement and both reached their apotheosis in the law permitting abortion on demand (Ann Barbeau Gardiner, Review of Christine Rosen's book *Preaching Eugenics,* *New Oxford Review,* October 2006, pp 42-45).

A science teacher, Harry Hamilton Laughlin, who received a Doctor in Science (D.Sc) from Princeton, was a principal advocate of sterilization. He published in 1914 a document called a *Model Eugenical Sterilization Law* authorizing the sterilization of the "socially inadequate" who were "a menace to society." The menace included "the feebleminded, insane, criminalistic, epileptic, inebriate, diseased, blind, deaf, deformed, and dependent." The law in the state of Virginia declared that "heredity plays an important part in the transmission of insanity, idiocy, imbecility, epilepsy and crime…." Carrie Buck, a 17-year-old Virginia girl had the honor of being the first person picked to be sterilized according to Virginia law. The *Buck v. Bell* decision, by the way, has never been overruled.

Harry Hamilton Laughlin was indeed "an honorable man," as Antony says of Brutus. Among those who honored him for his ideas, besides Justice Holmes, was the Nazi Government which adopted a law in 1933 that borrowed from his *Model Law* and was the legal basis for sterilizing more than 350,000 Germans. Laughlin was awarded an honorary degree from Heidelberg University in 1936 in recognition for his ideas in "the science of racial cleansing" (Alex Wellerstein, "Harry Lauglin's Modle Sterilization Law", http://www.people. fas.harvard.edu/~wellerst/lauglin/,2006). Incidentally, Laughlin was an epileptic and hence a candidate for sterilization under his own law. Bad ideas are the whispers by the seducers to the seduced about nature and society in the way that Iago's whispers poisoned Othello about Desdemona's virtue.

Bad Theories of Marxist Inspiration

Two theories of law that appeared first in law schools and then received wider dissemination in Western culture during the '70s and '80s were the feminist theory of law and that of the Critical Legal Studies Movement. Both theories, while Marxist in inspiration, did not appeal to the economic determinism and class warfare of orthodox Marxism. Still economics and class warfare are never completely out of the picture in both theories.

In feminist theory of law, the Marxist dialectic of opposites and oppression was held to be the opposition between the sexes, with men as the oppressors of women, not contingently and individually, but as historically necessary and as a class. Law, especially the laws of marriage and those of the bearing and the educating of children, was the instrument of women's oppression. The materialism of feminist law, while not a matter of emphasis, appeared in an odd way when feminist law professor Catherine MacKinnon claimed that there was no difference in kind between a husband and wife having sex and a rapist taking sex (Cited and quoted by Christina Sommers, "Hard Line Feminists Guilty of Ms.-Representation," *Wall Street Journal*, 11/17/91, Editorial page). Physiologically and materialistically speaking, the acts looked similar. Penetration and, therefore, symbolic stabbing, the physical expression of man's oppression of woman, took place in both events. The fact of the complementarity of men and women for reproduction and education of the species cuts no ice in the face of exotic lunacy.

The point about law in feminist theory is that law is power, force, and ultimately violence. According to the theory, the "rule of law" is rhetorical. Such rhetoric masks law itself, made as it is by men, as oppression of women.

Critical common sense realism says that if law is power or force, then it is not law. Law is rule by reason or it is not law. So called legal realists may sniff at what they regard as naiveté, but in their rhetoric and in their own proposals of law, they must make believe that law is rooted in reason and fairness.

Just as the schools of theology had their love affair with the Marxism of liberation theology, so too did the schools of law with the Marxism of the Critical Legal Studies movement, especially at Yale and Harvard. It too had a Latin American Theorist in the person of Brazilian, Roberto Mangabeira Unger. The name "Critical Legal Studies" refers to the Frankfurt school of Critical Marxism which, as we saw in our chapter on the behavioral sciences, was an unhappy combination of Marxism and Freudianism, and it was unhappy because the Frankfurters combined two theories both of which claimed to be scientific and were not; and both of which failed in the practical order just as much as they failed in the theoretical order.

Western, especially American, law, say the Critical Legal Studies theorists, is the instrument of liberal materialistic capitalism which alienates workers from their work and causes the despair which follows from that alienation. Private property and illegitimate hierarchies are those features of liberal capitalism that most require reform, if not revolution, into an arrangement of communitarian ownership. The law and constitution must be changed to reflect that revolution.

Critical Legal Studies theorists claim to diverge from orthodox Marxism in that they reject historical determinism or inevitability. By 1989 it was clear that this feature of orthodox Marxism, i.e., the inevitable development toward socialism, had been falsified. They diverge equally from the crass materialism of orthodox Marxism and tend to be influenced more profoundly by the early Marx of the *German Ideology,* a sort of spiritual Marxism, and by the cultural Marxism of Antonio Gramsci. This is to say that the conflict is not between economic classes but rather between ideas and ideological domination. Western ideas and culture must be subsumed and superseded by Third World ideas and culture, the culture of "the wretched of the earth," into a synthesis of international culture. This is accomplished through the capture of the cultural institutions such as the universities, law schools, museums, libraries and media. This has already happened in and to the West.

Law as force or coercion, or as the mask for the defense of private property (of whatever kind, ideas included) and illegitimate hierarchies will no longer be needed in the atmosphere of equality and multiculturalism. In that atmosphere people will just get along without law, without nations, without conflict. Law conceived as force is a bad idea because it is false. The elimination of law itself because it is thought to be force and, therefore oppression, is also a bad idea, not only because it is false but also because it is utopian. It is nowhere law because it belongs to nowhere man.

A Sound (i.e., True and Valid) Definition of Law

To get a good idea in the understanding of law, we must return to those thrilling days of yesteryear when the West was young, to the '60s, that is, to the 1260s, when a monk out of Naples and Paris said some things about the nature of law that can and will guide us out of the lunacy and reticulation of the Modern and Postmodern bad ideas. We speak of the definition of Law found in St. Thomas Aquinas' *Summa Theologiae*. Be warned, however, that because Aquinas was a medieval thinker, a Catholic theologian, and was non-scientific in the way Hobbes, Austin, Kelsen and Holmes would insist that he be, he is regarded by the cultural elite as not part of the legitimate debate on the concept of law. But this elite, when confronted with critical common sense realism and with sound arguments it is unable to defeat, banishes its adversaries, nay foes, to an historical reliquary that is beyond the pale of legitimate debate. We just don't know our place! But now to the best definition of law you will ever come across for its simplicity, its truth, and its validity.

St. Thomas says (in our translation) that law is "a rational command issued for the common good by those who have authority in the community and that is expressed publicly." Hence, law is not the will of the stronger, or the will of the sovereign or a prediction of what judges will do. It is a dictate of reason completed by an act of will. If law does not issue from reason, it is not law. Even the will of God is subject to God's reason in its enactments. Moslems,

Occamists and other voluntarists say otherwise, but theirs is an arbitrary God. Such an arbitrary God is not one worthy of belief and trust.

Law is for the common good, not the good of the sovereign; whether the sovereign be the ruler, the majority, or the minority. Law is an act of reason and desire that aims at the satisfaction of all the citizens subject to the law. Private aims and private goods receive their legitimacy from the common good. If law does not aim at the common good, it is not law but preferential treatment.

Not everyone in a given society has the authority to make law. That authority belongs either to the whole people or to the public personage who represents the whole people and has care of the whole people. If the law is to be the instrument of education for the citizens, it must possess *coercive power* to be effective. That power is vested in the whole people or in some public personage whose duty it is to command, permit, and prohibit the citizens and to execute penalties on wrongdoers.

Evidently in this definition of law, there is no conflict with law as an expression of reason and force or coercion. St. Thomas, along with the boys and girls on the stoop, understands that there are some people who can be governed and persuaded by reason but that there are others who cannot and must be ruled by force. It is also evident that the proper aim of law is to direct and educate the citizens so that each develops and contributes his own proper virtue. But since there are those, for whatever the motive or cause, who harm themselves and others through the various tendencies (i.e., vices, such as envy, lust or greed) they choose to exercise, then such persons must in the first place be educated by the fear of punishment and, in the second, to be actually punished for their crime.

Of course one of the worst of the bad ideas of our time is that criminals are not responsible for their crimes but that they are helpless victims of either their biology or their society. If the problem of crime is thought, by the cultural elite, to be a reduction to biology or society and not to the vices and choices of individuals, then they will propose sterilization or abortions for bad biology and reeducation and rehabilitation for bad society. Crimes traced to bad deterministic biology involve some punishment to individuals as we learned from the *Buck v. Bell* decision. But if crime is traced to social determinism because of its economic and political arrangements, then the criminal is a victim of society such that punishment is out of order altogether. In the case of biological determinism, the criminal's genes made him do it; in that of social determinism, society made him do it. On the part of the criminal, no choice, no responsibility, no crime, no punishment! The professors of law have gone beyond talk of rehabilitation to talk of no punishment at all.

On the other hand, for some of the cultural elite such as departed lawyer, William Kunstler, novelist Norman Mailer, and *New York Times* journalist, Tom Wicker, criminals are heroes, a vanguard courageously battling an oppressive and unjust society. For Kunstler and Wicker, we have but to remember the Attica Prison riot of 1970 and their roles in it. As for Mailer, there are his exquisite efforts to free murderer Jack Henry Abbot in 1981, because Abbot's writing ability so impressed him. Abbot repaid Mailer's tenderness for him and Mailer's sympathy for social order by murdering again. Mailer is a marquis example of a Brooklynite who lost his way in the tortured convolutions of his puerile imagination. The glow from his ego dimmed the Brooklyn street lights which enlighten the stoops where critical common sense realism abides. You can put the boy in Brooklyn, but you can't put Brooklyn in the boy. Nor can we forget that Kunstler, Mailer and Wicker had their supporters in such institutions as The American Civil Liberties Union and *The New York Times*, along with those precious intellectuals in the law schools and universities who shared their "noble" ideas.

As Edmund Burke said of some of the intellectuals at the time of the French Revolution (1789), we can say of ours:

> *They could not bear the punishment of the mildest laws on the greatest criminals. The slightest severity of justice made their flesh*

creep. The very idea that war existed in the world disturbed their repose. Military glory was no more, with them, than a splendid infamy. Hardly would they hear of self-defense which they reduced within such bounds, as to leave it no defense at all ("Letter to a Noble Lord," p. 410 in the Harvard Classics edition).

This necessary digression on crime and punishment was entertained so as to illustrate that reason and force are not incompatible in the governance of human beings. Force is rational in order that vices might be held in check and innocence protected. For those who do not leave others in peace, fear of punishment is the discipline of laws, a discipline which can only be effective if punishments are actually administered.

The last feature of St. Thomas' four part definition is that in order for commands to be laws they must be promulgated, that is, they must be expressed publicly. If they are not, they are private commands, that is, privileges not laws. In order that laws be binding, they must be applied to those persons who are to be governed by them. This application is made known to them through promulgation.

Civil Rights of Criminals and Terrorists

In *Don Quixote*, Part I Chapter 22, Cervantes relates the episode wherein the quite mad "Knight of the Woeful Countenance" comes across a chain gang of men sentenced and forced to serve in the King's gallies. Sancho, the Knight's squire, informs him that they are rogues sentenced by the law for their misdeeds. To which Don Quixote replies, "They are forced because they do not go of their own free will. If this be so, they come within the scope of my duty which is to hinder violence and oppression and to succor all people in misery." After he frees them from their chains, the convicts celebrate their liberty by turning on their liberator and stoning him for his chivalrous act. Reflecting sadly on this moment of his madness, the Don regrets to find himself,

Sancho, Rozinante, his horse and Sancho's donkey "so barbarously repaid by those whom he had so highly obliged."

Poor Don Quixote was loco in a noble and charming way. But his mad act did not unleash mayhem only on himself and his friend but on his immediate society as well. While Cervantes does not say so explicitly, his intention is clear. The freed convicts were free to commit further crimes. The lawyers and judges who fight for the rights of criminals in the all-atoning name of civil liberties are foolish and mad in the objective madness of bad ideas. And when their flights of fancy desert them, their arrogance sustains them. Consider, for example, the description of a lecture given by Professor of Law, Monroe Freedman, announced in the Hofstra University 2007 Calendar of events: "In Praise of Unethical Conduct by Lawyers — Deceiving Other People, Lying to Judges, and Other Moral [sic] Behavior." Perhaps Professor Freedman is being ironic.

Don Quixote at the end of part II of the novel recognizes his foolishness and madness on his deathbed in the so-called reversal of Sancho's "realism" and his own "idealism." Sancho pleads with him to return to the quest. The Knight of the Woeful Countenance replies: "*En los nidos de antaño, no hay pajaros de hogaño.*" (There are no birds of today in the nests of yesteryear.) Such critical common sense realism is not to be found behind the fevered brows of the lawyers and supporters of criminal rights legislation and now even terrorist rights legislation. This is to say that foreign terrorists are to have the same constitutional protections as American citizens accused of the kind of crimes processed through the criminal justice system. Foreign terrorists, therefore, are to be accorded rights protection created by the criminal-rights Supreme Court decisions of the 1960's. No kidding! The *Hamdan v. Rumsfeld* decision of June 2006 follows illogically but inexorably from such cases as *Escobedo v. Illinois* (1964), *Miranda v. Arizona* (1966), *United States v. Wade* (1967), *Gilbert v. California* (1967), and *Mempa v. Rhay* (1967). But Hamdan goes beyond the criminal rights decisions. It challenges the authority of the Constitution itself, and the limits, therefore, on judicial authority and the very sovereignty of the

American nation. It does so by the seductive oratory of "human rights" and by the appeal to an international combination of the United Nations, international tribunals, nongovernmental organizations (NGO's), multi-national corporations, and bureaucrats of nation states who share the same internationalist ideology, the residue of Marxist utopian folly.

Escobedo treated the right to counsel in the period before trial. The Court was concerned about abuses of police methods of investigation and this concern led to a more complete treatment of the issue in *Miranda*. The war for criminal rights was stepped up as regards the use of confessions obtained by police interrogation without informing the suspects of their right to remain silent and to have counsel. Furthermore, the so-called "exclusionary rule" forbids evidence obtained in violation of the Fourth Amendment from being used against a defendant in court. In *Mapp v Ohio* (1961) the prohibition on "illegally" obtained evidence was strengthened further. Such steps in the protection of the rights of citizens by protecting the rights of criminals were not taken without controversy. According to Herman Prittchett in his book *The American Constitution*, the Brits do not accept it. An expert authority on evidence, John Wigmore, stands against it and Justice Benjamin Cardozo argued that it was not right that "the criminal should go free because the constable had blundered" (Pritchett, p. 435).

This madness was further encouraged by the inability of American courts to define obscenity and pornography. That inability led to two results: the first was that the courts could not stop the proliferation of obscenity, pornography and even borderline sedition, such as flag-burning and "celebrities" advancing the cause of America's enemies; the second was that the legal establishment has defended obscenity and pornography in the name of the constitutionally guaranteed right of free speech.

In the most excellent sermons of the elite, bad ideas are exalted in the catechism of rights and in the policy of the state. The "aeronauts" of the law schools and the courts fly very high in putting on the follies which caricature the process of the law. But we dare not laugh too loudly or too publicly. Lawyers run America, a country that used to be a regime of the laws. (Ordinary citizens used to serve in the Congress not just lawyers.) As legislators, lawyers write the laws; as judges, lawyers interpret the laws; as public administrators and private practitioners, lawyers execute the laws. Judge-made law (Juristocracy) is simply a subset of lawyer made law. *"Res ipsa loquitur."* (The matter [i.e., the rule of lawyers and not the rule of law] speaks for itself.)

Litigating for Power and Profit

Civil law, and not just criminal law, has its own brand of lunacy, the paradigm case for which is the $3 million verdict, including punitive damages, for the woman who burned herself in the act of removing the lid from her McDonald's coffee cup upon leaving the drive-thru window. Hooray for the high tech ambulance chasers (by virtue of current media) who take on the big bad manufacturers and corporations *to fight* for the little guy or gal!

The American legal system permits contingency fees and extensive pre-trial discovery procedures. Contingency fees free the plaintiffs from paying their lawyers if the suit does not succeed. By lessening the cost to plaintiffs who sue, contingency fees generate more lawsuits. Extensive and extended pre-trial discovery procedures are so expensive and time-consuming that depositions go on for months and years before trials begin. Discovery procedures of this kind discourage defendants from undergoing them or from going to trial. Rather they encourage defendants to settle with plaintiffs on terms which favor the plaintiffs. But this generosity toward plaintiffs and their lawyers on the part of American tort jurisprudence has not only redistributed the wealth of such industries as those of tobacco, drugs, asbestos, and silicone breast implant products, but also has reached into the pocketbooks of the general public in its having to pay additionally for the cost of companies' doing business. The area where the public is aware of trial lawyers fleecing it is in the cost of health care, which is swollen by the malpractice insurance physicians must pay to practice medicine. The lawyers have truly stuck it to the doctors along with the corporations. But the trial lawyer cartel pleads its case as fighting for the rights of victims of corporate negligence and medical malpractice. All that one has to do to get a sense of lawyerly beneficence and compassion is to listen to the commercials of law firms on radio and television.

The asbestos, tobacco, and silicone breast implant litigations are instructive about the depth of trial lawyer efforts for the common good and compassion for the huddled masses yearning to get rich and to make a few bucks for themselves as well. It so happens that in the asbestos litigations the law firms have been found to be, as they say in the trade, double-dipping and engaged in fraud (*Wall Street Journal*, December 5, 2006, Opinion). They do this by filing claims for a single client against several trust funds that have been set up by such companies as Johns Manville, Celotex, and Bethlehem Steel to deal with asbestos liabilities.

In the case of tobacco, the law is now such that the companies bear full responsibility for lung cancer and emphysema incurred by smokers. Irrespective of being warned by common opinion, doctors and physical educators long before warnings were given on packages of tobacco products, the individual smokers bear no responsibility for bringing on their sicknesses.

As far as breast implant litigation is concerned, we learn that the chivalrous trial lawyers obtained a $3.2 billion settlement in 1999 with Dow Corning Corporation which found it had to declare bankruptcy as a procedure to halt litigation. Now we learn as of this writing, that silicone breast implants have returned to the delight of guys and gals everywhere because an American "study" has found that there is no connection between breast implants and breast disease. (Memo to Dow Corning, Re: Truth. Oops!) If, however, a European "study" finds otherwise, then we can expect another round of litigation. The lawsuits are driven, critical common sense realists would say, by greedy lawyers and equivocal science. And the public pays. In legal terms, *Contra factum, non est argumentum,* (Against fact, there is no argument) as they say in Bensonhurst.

Civil Rights and Civil Wrongs

The Supreme Court decisions in *Brown v. Board of Education of Topeka* (1954) and in *Bolling v. Sharpe* (1954) rooted in the 14th Amendment of the US Constitution prohibited official segregation in schools at first, but then in any public facility under government supervision. The success of these decisions which repudiated discrimination sparked the Civil Rights Act of 1964, the Voting Rights Act of 1965 and the Fair Housing Act of 1968. These strides in the march toward social justice and equality began to side-step the overt language of the laws made by prior decisions. In *Green v. County School Board of New Kent County* (1968), the Court shifted the language of *Brown* prohibiting racial segregation and discrimination by government to the demand for integration. The shift in language and policy continued in the *Swann v Charlotte-Mecklenburg Board of Education* (1971), a busing case, requiring students to be assigned by race, not for its own sake but as a remedy for previous racial discrimination.

The policy of affirmative action had been broached earlier in 1961 under President John F. Kennedy's executive order 10925. The words "affirmative action" in that order meant at that time eliminating racial discrimination by requiring government contractors to open up opportunity for jobs through public notices on one hand and eliminating nepotism and favoritism on the other. This meaning of the words "affirmative action" as a result of subsequent Supreme Court decisions becomes "preferential treatment" in effect. Those decisions were *Griggs v. Duke Power Company* (1971), *Regents of California v. Bakke* (1978) and *United Steelworkers v. Weber* (1979). There was no longer any need to prove that preferred blacks had actually been victims of racial discrimination and that rejected whites had discriminated or received benefit from discrimination. In employment and in education, race, despite the protests of the framers and supporters of theses decisions notwithstanding, became the decisive factor for acceptance or rejection.

In 1982 the *Plyer v. Doe* decisions declared that the 14th Amendment clause of the US Constitution requires state governments to provide free public education to illegal aliens thereby blurring the difference between citizens and non-citizens. In the face of the doctrine of rights, fundamental political distinctions are negated while new rights blossom, not *ex nihilo*, of course, but on the fertile ground of the 14th Amendment. And in 2003 the *Grutter v. Bollinger* decision said that the University of Michigan law School could use race as a factor in admissions so that the School could achieve, in the words of its imaginative proponents on the Court, a "critical mass" of a particular racial group. Americans had to be reminded that they had already said goodbye to the idea of a color-blind society in prior civil rights legislation.

In that same year (2003) the sacred doctrines of equality and rights applied to homosexuality according to the *Lawrence v. Texas* decision. This decision in turn provided the rationale for the Supreme Court of the state of Massachusetts to declare a right to same sex marriage.

In the *Roe v. Wade* decision of 1973, abortion-on-demand was declared a constitutional right thereby overturning the abortion laws of the states. This decision gave women the sovereign power to choose between the life and death of their offspring in the early stages of his or her development. We do not mean a *potential* human person but an *actual* human person in the early stages of development. This mother of all rights gave birth to another decision, *Stenberg v. Carhart* (2000) which declared partial birth abortion a constitutional right. After this decision, lawyers and "philosophers" no longer needed to pretend or to argue that the fetus was neither human nor a person. The humanity of the child was evident. The "birth" in partial birth abortion demonstrates the humanity and individuality of the child. Its mother now had the right to kill it or to have it killed by a cooperating physician. Critical common sense realists wonder why this medical procedure of dismembering a human child, a paradigm of civil rights litigation, is never presented on any of the TV science shows. The 2007 decision restricting partial birth abortion, surprisingly, is a partial return to common sense and to humanity.

When the follies of the law baffle understanding, they move into the domain of a grotesque carnival where derisive and dismissive ridicule is no longer appropriate. The carnival has moved beyond ridicule. It engenders horror and disgust. It is a scene aptly depicted in the paintings of Hieronymus Bosch. The voices from the stoop hush for a moment of silence.

CHAPTER SIX:
Art, Beauty and Technology

Nature and Art

Among the things that exist, there are those which exist by nature and those which exist through art and technology. This classification, albeit very wide, is nevertheless correct. Putting aside the issue of whether the things which exist by nature are created by an omnipotent God or whether nature itself is their cause, we can say for certain that the things which exist by art are caused or created not *ex nihilo* but by human beings using the materials that nature in general provides. They do so by virtue of that act of the mind called the imagination working on the natural things that they perceive; then by reordering or putting those natural things together in ways in which they are not found in nature.

Dreams, daydreams, and nightmares, as well as the products of art, whatever the art may be, are the results of the imagination. Centaurs and unicorns do not exist in nature, but horses and men do, as do horses and horns. Centaurs and unicorns are mythical animals produced by the human imagination. They are dependent for their composition on natural things that are perceived and remembered. Faust, the character and the play, does not exist in nature but ambitious men and language do. *Faust*, the play, is composed of the language produced by the imagination of the poet Goethe operating on acts of human beings, that is, selling their souls for "knowledge" or for the kisses of Helen of Troy. Michelangelo's statue of Moses does not exist in nature, but the marble does, as did the person, Moses, about whom the artist had read and learned. The various arts are modes of imitation (*Mimesis*). What they imitate or represent is not nature but actions. As Aristotle says: "All human happiness or misery takes the form of action" (*Poetics, 6, 1450a, 17-19*). As forms of poetry, the various arts imitate action. Francis Slade, commenting on Aristotle, says:

The narrative arts presuppose the ontological priority of ends to purposes because without that priority there is nothing to be revealed about the adequacy or inadequacy of human purposes to the completeness of a human life, for in action a human being "purposes" the realization of his life as a whole, complete in itself. Life as action is a whole, and it is the presence of an end that makes it a whole. Stories imitate actions by being themselves wholes that represent the manifestations of ends in action (Francis Slade, "On the Ontological Priority of Ends and its Relevance to the Narrative Arts," Beauty, Art, and the Polis, ed. Alice Ramos. Washington D.C.: The Catholic University Press of America, 2000, p. 67).

The ontological priority of ends is not deterministic; for human beings can act in concert with or contrary to nature.

Nature is not the complex of all the objects of experience. Nor is it the existence of things as determined by universal laws. Both of these formulations are offered by the philosopher Immanuel Kant in his *Prolegomena to Any Future Metaphysics* (1783, pp.14 & 16). Both formulations, however, make nature subject to and dependent upon one part of it which came along late in nature's history, namely, human nature. Also, nature is not just the physical world, usually the outdoors, including all living things. Rather 1) it is what exists for the most part, and 2) is normative for the things that exist (Natural Law). The adjective "natural" captures this second sense of nature. The nature of a thing is the end for the sake of which the thing exists. This is to say that nature is ordered by goals or ends (Teleology). The ends of nature are distinct from human intention or purpose, although human purposes are part of the ends of nature.

Technology

The part that does not exist by nature is the part that exists by art. And what is art if not the act of making things, in the first place, and making them well, in the second place. A well-made thing performs as it is intended or as it is supposed to perform. This conception of art takes in not only the finished work, e.g., the statue of Moses, Chartres Cathedral, the Mona Lisa, Beethoven's Ninth Symphony, but also the tools used to make them, such as the hammers and chisels, the paint and the canvas and the musical instruments. Technology, then, is a sub-category of art. It produces the tools that produce the work of art. Technology is the servant or handmaid of art. It extends human perception and action.

While technology is a tool and a servant of human art, it can and has become a master. This is its danger. For if it becomes a master, then its makers become its servants. Operating as it does at the interstices of human activity, it causes and changes that activity, such that it is not so easy to differentiate between causes and effects. Science fiction abounds with the fact that machines control our lives. This is especially so with the "machines" of information technology. And because these machines are electronic, they are not even machines in the old sense of the term which still required human work to move and operate them. The electronic instruments abstract from human effort. They are examples of "action at a distance." It is true that they must be "programmed," but after that, they operate on their own with just the push of a button, a wave or clap of the hand, or a stroll across a light beam. With the exception of the indomitable few of independent mind and action, "i Life" has become the life of the average human being, what with cell phones, the computer, i pods, mp3's, pda's, text messaging, e-mail, and the internet. These instruments of information and communication do develop the tendency through their abuse to trivialize and subvert the very human activities that they were intended to enhance and improve such as seeing, listening, remembering, thinking, speaking and writing.

The electronic spider has us caught in the World Wide Web. The promise of leisure is both made and broken. Only those people of independent mind can take that leisure to practice a human life through science, art and philosophy and not waste it on frivolous activity such as playing with video games and indulging in pornography, slave-producing addictions.

What and where is the place of beauty in all this? Beauty means and is defined as that quality of a thing, person, or object which makes it "pleasing to perception." A beautiful thing, whether it exists by nature, as a woman, or a flower; or exists by art, as a painting, sculpture or a concerto, is pleasing to see, hear, smell, taste, or touch, with the emphasis on seeing and hearing. No matter how multiculturalist, relativist, or subjectivist someone may be ideologically, this is everyone's idea of beauty. People may differ — but not that much — as to the things they regard as beautiful but the idea of beauty is the same for everyone.

The Criteria for Beautiful Things

And what is a thing of beauty? For everyone, except the 20th century's cultural establishment, the makers of fashion, whose aim is to dictate and distort in the name of originality, novelty, or just for the hell of it — a thing of beauty is a thing of nature or a work of art that possesses "integrity," "harmony or proportionality," and "splendor of form." Integrity refers to the object's unity of parts. Whether the object be a woman, a painting, a poem, a symphony, a sculpture or a building, the parts fit and cling together in a unity. The opposite is disunity, or as the scientistas call it "randomness."

The manner in which the parts fit together and are made for each other is their "harmony" or "proportionality." The plurality and variety of parts are proportionate and agreeable to each other. The opposite is disorder and discord. We speak not only of musical compositions but also of any beautiful thing such that its witness, observer, or hearer can say: "Yes! It is fitting."

The truth of the thing, an ideal of what it is supposed to be is the thing's "splendor of form." And form does not mean shape. It means the essence of the thing. It is form in the Platonic sense so that whether a building be Classical, Gothic, Islamic, Romanesque, or *Art Decoratif*; whether a painting be a Giotto, a Vermeer, a Velasquez, or a Renoir; a piece of music be by Vivaldi, Bach, Mozart, or Debussy; a poem by Virgil, Dante, Milton, or Eliot; a sculpture by Phidias, Michelangelo, Rodin or Mestrovic — the truth or essence of the thing shines forth. In other words, what the thing is supposed to be comes through. The particular and individual work of art expresses in its own way an ideal form.

Modernist Art and the Culture War

Since the Platonic form has long been discarded by the nominalistic culture warriors, there is no ideal form to guide and restrain either them or the artists. Objectivity and universality are declared non-existent. Only subjectivity and radical individuality remain for the artist and for the spectator. No criteria of beauty or standards of taste exist for either of them. Beauty departs with the denial of objectivity and universality. No reasons can be given or taught for why a work of art is good or beautiful. No appeals to integrity, harmony or splendor of form! The "truth" of the work is the artist's subjectivity — his unfettered and, therefore, "free" idea of things. For the spectator, "truth" is whatever he likes. The value of a work of art is whatever the curators of museums say it is and whatever art-dealers and art-buyers agree upon as art. We note with interest that a painting entitled "White Center" by Mark Rothko was sold at Sotheby's auction in May 2007 for $73 million. This "masterpiece" consists of three horizontal but unequal swaths of paint with the white swath in the middle. The event is a perfect example of what we are talking about. And none dare call it a disgrace.

The aim, therefore, of modernist art is not truth or beauty but originality, novelty, the "courage" and "honesty" to distort and deconstruct nature and tradition. Antoni Gaudi's Church of the Sagrada Familia in Barcelona is modern, whereas Frank Gehry's Guggenheim Museum in Bilbao is Modernist. For Modernist art no mimesis or imitation of anything will do. Its "courage" and "honesty" is the distinctive courage and honesty of modernity — the courage to be me (in societies, of course, which have become caricatures of democracy). This is unmitigated drivel, but it is drivel endorsed and enshrined, unfortunately, in such popular songs as Frank Sinatra's "My Way," Sammy Davis Jr.'s "I've Gotta be Me," Billy Joel's "My Life," and Jon Bon Jovi's "It's My Life." It is unfortunate because the drivel has had the result that the public finds difficult to resist — the enshrinement of the self-validation of egoism expressed in those songs, especially so in the "culture" of the "Me-Century." Songs like these are the vehicles of seduction. As we said in the introduction: "The long march of radical democratization has led the seduced to imagine themselves as independent and unique." Hence they willingly embrace the bad ideas expressed by the words "my way" and "my life," by which they are seduced. Who cares whether it's *your* way or *your* life: Come around and talk to us if your way is the *right* way or *your* life is a life worth living for a human being and is not that of a beast, a scoundrel or a smart-ass.

Further evidence of the willing seduction of the folks is the way they have accepted and even approved of the "moneyfication" and "showbusnification" of sports. While they complain, but only mildly, about its "moneyfication," they have "no problem" with its "showbusnification." The makers of opinion have seen to it that the term "celebrity" is reserved for the gods and goddesses of entertainment — the show-biz people. Thus the public tolerates the "showboating" of the athletes, on and off the field or court; the gimmickry of the telecasts such as the use of the zoom lens, the sub-titles with the scores of other games and sports besides the one being telecast (distracting the fans from the game at hand while pretending to keep them informed); and the split-second change of images so characteristic in the filming of Rock and Rap videos which is exalted with the name "montage." Then, of course, there are the recent half-time shows of the Super Bowl — professional football's flashiest event — with such Rock stars as Michael Jackson, Justin Timberlake *cum* Janet Jackson, the Rolling Stones, and Prince prancing across a stage. To paraphrase the Bandito in the movie *The Treasure of Sierra Madre* (1948): sports "don't need no stinking" Rock stars to decorate them. Nor do they need the tarted up cheerleaders of the Dallas Cowboys. What ever happened to the traditional half-time show such as performed by the Florida A&M Marching Band?

As far as politics is concerned, it has been a part of show-biz for a long time, certainly from the era of John F. Kennedy onward (circa 1960). Since then the word politics refers more to partisanship and to running for office than to governing. Again television has been the vehicle, but TV itself is also the message (with a tip of the hat to Marshall McLuhan). But to say so about politics and TV has become a cliché, so we will say no more about them here.

God forbid that we say anything about the "music" that formed the souls of the young over the last 50 years, i.e., Rock, and for the last 15, Hip Hop. When Allan Bloom, following Plato, dared to describe and interpret certain kinds of music — in Bloom's case, Rock, as orgiastic, anti-rational, cruel and born of coarse sensibilities (*The Closing of the American Mind*, 1987, pp. 68-81), he incurred not only the wrath of the university youths, but also that of the entertainment establishment and their spokesmen in the media. How dare he question the most intimate possession of the young — their music! We tread lightly here, for we do not want to trespass on sacred ground. Furthermore, we acknowledge the musical charm of some kinds of rock such as classic soft rock performed by The Eagles, Chicago, Fleetwood Mac, and The Bee Gees. Bloom ran the risk of having his arguments dismissed — that is, on the failure of higher education to uphold democracy and enrich the souls of students — because of his unnuanced criticism of Rock. Didn't Bloom know that the "true" message of the music of the '60s – whose devotees are not only the young but also the not so young, since many have now reached the age of 60 – was not sex, drugs, and Rock and Roll but rather civil rights, peace, and love. At least that is what we have been told by such oppressed rockers as Bob Dylan, Crosby, Stills, and Nash, Joni Mitchell, John Lennon, The Who, The Grateful Dead, The Doors and their acolytes. It is fun to imagine what Plato would have said if he were present at the Woodstock or Isle of Wight (1970) to hear the rock version of Lydian mode music (that is, music of passionate frenzy); "Such emotion without the tab."

We will be more discrete because we wish to be heard over the "wall of sound" of Rock, its lovers, its critics and its cultured defenders. What is more, we almost hesitate to call attention to how the public's cooperation with its seduction by taste-makers is evident in what current TV shows both the public and the taste-makers have popularized such as "American Idol," "Survivor" and "Desperate Housewives," not to speak of the symbiosis between the rockers and their fans. It is no accident that the pinnacle of celebrity status in the century of image is the image of the rock star rather than the reality of Medal of Honor winners. It is a good thing that in an authentic free society, other kinds of entertainment are available for those with less manipulable tastes.

The Revolt of the Unnatural and Anti-natural

What we have said in the previous paragraphs about nature, art, beauty, and technology is common sensical, traditional and pre-modern. So what are the problems? We have already mentioned some things to indicate what those problems are. Because of the culture war in the 20th Century, the traditional ideas of nature, art, beauty and technology have become so controversial as to have led to their rejection and to a revolution in the culture which came to be called Modernity or Modernist. The war is a revolt against these traditional or premodern ideas. The revolt is being led by the cultural elite who work in the universities, the museums, the art schools, the law schools, the foundations, and the media; the last of which is the name of the vehicle through which the revolutionary propaganda is transmitted, especially through telecommunications.

Take, for example, the prosaic ideas "natural" and "unnatural" and then the not so prosaic idea "anti-natural." In the domain of sex, the cultural revolutionaries have declared that there are acts which are neither natural nor unnatural, neither normal nor abnormal. This sophistic dodge is the attempt to achieve liberation through sexual excess, as is the case with the ideas of such gurus as Wilhelm Reich and Alfred Kinsey mentioned in our chapter on the behavioral sciences. The revolutionaries repeat the denial of the natural-unnatural difference when speaking about some areas of biological research and medical practice such as cloning and human embryo-killing stem cell research. The "erasure" of the difference between what is natural and what is unnatural has been achieved through the abuse of technology. Adultery, sodomy and bestiality have long existed, but they were publicly proscribed. Now they have become acceptable; and two of the three, adultery and sodomy even glorified. Natural is, we are told, as natural does.

Most recently, bestiality has received the endorsement of Princeton Philosophy Professor, Peter Singer, when he suggested that "humans should consider breeding with chimpanzees" (*The New Criterion*, February, 2007, p. 3). Perhaps he means breeding by *in vitro* fertilization but somehow we don't think so. We suggest in this regard that Professor Singer should do a test himself so as to discover the charms of a wild and crazy chimp. The Marquis de Sade, the hero of revolutionary and radical Enlightenment thought, would be proud of Singer who is Princeton's Dr. Moreau of *The Island of Dr. Moreau* book (1896) and movie (1977) fame. Revolutionary sex for a revolutionary century! Of course, bestiality is beyond unnatural; it is anti-natural. For those who wish to delve more deeply into this subject, we recommend its "tasteful" treatment in a "film" called *Zoo* (2007) by Director Robinson Devor.

We await some member of the ruling elite, someone as courageous as Dr. Singer-Moreau, to recommend another *avant-garde* act besides bestiality; forbidden, but one that is at least an act within the human species. We speak of making love to the dead — necrophilia. It too has had its devotees who, poor souls, have had to live under the heel of the oppressive ideas of nature and tradition. Together with bestiality, it too would have its own website on the internet entitled "In Bed with the Dead." Since some pornography is artistic, necrophilia could be portrayed, again "tastefully" (a favorite word of the tastemakers) through the World Wide Web, if it isn't already. We suspect that an activist rights group will be formed and will be called "The Necrophilic Liberation Front" (The NLF). Lest anyone think that forming a rights group for necrophilia is beyond the pale, it was only a short while ago that sex with children and child pornography was regarded as beyond the pale. Yet a group already exists, NAMBLA (The North American Man-Boy Love Association); and its freedom of speech is even defended by the American Civil Liberties Union, a civil rights organization and a prominent member of the cultural elite. We can only wonder if NAMBLA gets the ministrations of the ACLU because it is a prep school for Gay Rights groups. The rhetoric of anti-racism, anti-sexism, anti-homophobia, and anti-fascism is the mask worn to disguise their exquisite tastes.

Consequently, there should be no objection to necrophilia. No greater love can be bestowed on the dead than to make love to them. If the culture warriors from Robert Mapplethorpe to Madonna want to push envelopes, where "pushing the envelope" means acting contrary to nature and the moral law, again in the name of "honesty," then by all means, they should push all the way. After all, chant the culture warriors, who's to say what's natural or unnatural; moral or immoral? They believe that morality is a matter of *who* (subjectivity) says rather than *what* (objectivity) says. The ambiguity of sophisticated Postmodernity is erased by the wisdom of "anything goes." If anything goes, then *anything* goes. And all's well in cuckoo land. That there is a price for the largess of "anything goes" has not occurred to the culture warriors. But it has occurred to people like the Roman poet, Horace and the Victorian writer, Rudyard Kipling. We thank our friend and colleague, Frank Slade, a long time Brooklynite originally from Virginia, for calling our attention to these readings. Horace warns "You can drive nature out with a pitchfork, but it always comes back, and breaking in unexpectedly is victorious over your perverse contempt" (*Epistles*, I, 10, 24-25).

Kipling, that benighted old "racist," "colonialist," and "imperialist" puts it a bit more colorfully in *The Gods of the Copybook Headings* (1919) when he cautioned against violating nature:

As it will be in the future,

it was at the birth of Man—

There are only four things certain

since Social Progress began: —

That the Dog returns to his Vomit

and the Sow returns to her Mire,

And the burnt Fool's bandaged finger

goes wabbling back to the Fire;

And that after this is accomplished,

and the brave new world begins

When all men are paid for existing

and no man must pay for his sins,

As surely as Water will wet us,

as surely and Fire will burn

The Gods of the Copybook Headings

with terror and slaughter return!

Or, as Dr. Jerome Lejeune put it when asked as to whether AIDS represented a divine judgment of homosexual behavior: "God always forgives; man sometimes forgives; nature never forgives." And, thanks to the sexual revolution of the '60s, She has been paying us back for promiscuity by virtue of other sexually transmitted diseases, once under control and are now incurable; and still others, once barely known before but now also incurable.

The Battleground of the Culture War

The war as everyone knows or should know by this time occurs in and on the West. Non-westerners who are anti-westerners, such as Nehru, Pol Pot, Robert Mugabe and Mao-Tse-Tung were either educated in the West or taught by Western teachers, as in the case of Mao by the writings of Karl Marx.

The greatest of those teachers, a culture warrior of great intelligence and subtlety and who has the better claim on being the father of Modernity, rather than Descartes (1596-1650), is Niccolò Machiavelli. While he writes in a letter to Francesco Vettori, Letter # 137 (December 10,1513, Florence) that he is comfortable with the Ancient thinkers, his aim is to subvert them. The letter reveals that Uncle Nick is not just an advisor about *Realpolitik*, i.e., realism in politics. Rather, it turns out he himself is both the founding prince and the teacher of princes in the revolt against the Ancients. Indeed Machiavelli is the prince of Modernity.

> *On the coming of evening, I return to my house and enter my study; and at the door I take off the day's clothing, covered with mud and dust, and put on garments regal and courtly; and reclothed appropriately, I enter the ancient courts of ancient men, where, received by them with affection, I feed on that food which only is mine and which I was born for, where I am not ashamed to speak with them and to ask them the reason for their actions; and they in their kindness answer me; and for four hours of time I do not feel boredom, I forget every trouble, I do not dread poverty, I am not frightened by death; entirely I give myself over to them.*

This conversation with the Ancients suggests that Machiavelli is not, as we said, simply a political realist; not simply an Italian patriot in the face of the French occupation; not someone who has to be understood in his own time (as the cliché has it); not simply a partisan of the view that the end justifies the means; not a failed politician trying to make up for it by writing a political handbook on how to obtain and keep power; not just a teacher of evil as the Elizabethans understood him, e.g., Marlowe (*Dr. Faustus*) and Shakespeare (*Richard, III*); not a satirist of politics; but is rather a revolutionary philosopher rejecting the pre-modern view of things and their founding the modern view of things.

We are not saying that those interpretations are without merit, but they do not explain what we believe to be the deepest level of Machiavellianism. Nor are we saying that our interpretation is in any sense exhaustive. It is an attempt to suggest from a reading of some passages in *The Prince* (Written in 1513; published in 1532) that Machiavelli is the founder of Modernity in the pejorative sense. From those passages certain Machiavellian themes emerge. They are: 1) the acceptance of new things. To be new, i.e., modern, is to be good (*The Prince*, chap. III, xv); 2) the affirmation of power as also good (*The Prince*, chap., III, xi). Knowledge and thought are sub-categories of power. Marx, faithful Machiavellian that he was, put it simply and clearly when he said in his *Theses on Feuerbach* (1845): "The question whether human thinking can reach objective truth is not a question of theory but a *practical* question .... The dispute about the actuality or non-actuality of thinking, thinking isolated from practice, is purely a *scholastic* question ... (*Thesis*, 2); the philosophers have only *interpreted* the world in various ways; the point is, to *change* it." (*Thesis, 11*); 3) a revolutionary content within a traditional literary form, namely the form called the mirror for princes for which the model is *The Education of Cyrus* by Xenophon (The *Prince*, chap. XIV); 4) Machiavelli's conception of his teaching as a new code. In this respect, he sees himself as the new Moses establishing a new code of behavior. What he suggests ever so stealthily when speaking of armed prophets succeeding and unarmed prophets failing is that Jesus is an unarmed prophet and founder who succeeded after the Resurrection. Like Jesus, Machiavelli is an unarmed prophet who is, at the same time, the founder of a new system. Jesus is great because he exercises the greatest power, the power over minds (*The Prince*, chap. VI, xi); 5) the domain of nature characterized by chance (*fortuna*) can be controlled by virtue (*virtù*). The modern concept of knowledge and science, as control of nature by way of experimentation ("torturing nature"), finds its home at Machiavelli's. His idea of virtue is a shrinkage of the classical virtues of wisdom, courage, moderation and justice to shrewdness and boldness. No moderation and no justice! In the classical idea of virtue, virtue is the mean between the evils of excess and defect. For Machiavelli *virtù* is the mean between good and evil. Evil must be used well (*The Prince*, chap. VIII). "In the actions of all men and especially princes, where there is no court of appeal, the end is all that counts" (*The Prince*, chap., XVIII). As for *fortuna*, Machiavelli says:

> *I judge that it is better to be bold than cautious; for fortune is a woman and it is necessary in order to master her, beat her and hurt her. One sees she more submits to those who act boldly than to those who proceed more deliberately. Like a woman too, she is disposed to young men, for they are less cautious, more fierce, and command her with greater audacity. (The Prince, chap. XXV);*

6) politics creates morality. This is to say that moral laws can exist only after political society has been established and that political society cannot be established morally. Men like Pope Alexander VI reveal, according to Old Nick, the true features of the founders of political society and the ends-means relationship.

> *Alexander VI did nothing but deceive and never thought of anything else and always found some occasion for it...yet his deceptions were always successful for he was an expert in this field (The Prince, chap. XVIII)*

Although he [Alexander VI] did not aim so much at the greatness of the Church, as of the Duke [Caesar Borgia, Alexander's son], nonetheless the result of his activities was to increase the power of the Church.... His holiness Pope Leo, has thus found the present pontificate in a very strong position, whence we may hope that as his predecessors [Alexander VI] have made it powerful by force of arms, he will make it great and venerable by his kindness and infinite other virtues (The Prince, chap. XI).

Where does this place Jesus in Machiavelli's mind? The place is ambiguous and ambivalent. Machiavelli, like Jesus, is an unarmed prophet and founder who succeeds. But Machiavelli is the prophet and founder of modern thought and the rest of modernity which is the consequence of modern thought that he knows to be, "good Catholic" that he is, diametrically opposed to what Jesus is and what Jesus taught, namely the God-Man, the Incarnate Word, who taught a perfected form of the Mosaic Code, i.e., the moral law. Machiavelli dispenses with the moral law, as we have seen from chapters 11 and 18 of *The Prince* and replaces the God-Man with Chiron, the centaur, i.e., the beast-man, who was the legendary teacher of Achilles and other rulers (*The Prince*, chap. XVIII).

The other foe Machiavelli must vanquish in the establishment of Modernity is Plato, whom, like Jesus, he also does not mention by name. But it is Plato (especially in the *Republic*) that he has in mind, when he says:

I feel that I may be held presumptuous in what I have to say, if in my comments I do not follow the lines laid down by others, since, however, it has been my intention to write something which may be of use to the understanding reader, it has seemed wiser to me to follow the real truth of the matter rather than what we imagine it to be. For many authors have constructed republics and principalities that have never existed in practice and never could; for how we live is so different from how we ought to live that he who studies what ought to be done rather than what is done will learn the way to his downfall rather than to his preservation. A man striving in every way to be good will meet his ruin among the great number who are not good. Hence it is necessary for a prince, if he wishes to remain in power, to learn how not to be good and to use his knowledge or not use it as necessity demands (The Prince, chap. XV).

With that stroke of his pen, Nick takes care of Plato as well as Moses and Jesus, who are not only *his* foes but those of modernity. But Plato (Aristotle and Thomas Aquinas are critical Platonists) is not only a foe for constructing an ideal city in the *Republic*, but also because he affirms the reality of universal ideas: justice, truth, beauty and goodness being the most prominent and memorable. For Machiavelli and for the Modernity he founds, those ideas, as well as the other universals, are just words, fictions, whose meaning is given by the speakers of language, especially the ruling elite, as we pointed out in our chapter on education. The argument in Roman law that justice is natural, real, and universal and is the burden of the laws is a Platonic notion, captured neatly by Cicero in his *De Republica* (III, xxii, 3):

True law is right reason in agreement with Nature; it is of universal application, unchanging and everlasting; it summons to duty by its commands and averts from wrong-doing by its prohibitions.... We cannot be freed from its obligations by Senate or People, and we need not look outside ourselves for an expounder or interpreter of it. And there will not be different laws at Rome, at Athens or different laws now and in the future, but one eternal and unchangeable law will be valid for all nations and for all times....

This argument that there are natural laws discoverable and enacted according to human reason is fastened to Plato's idea of the Good which is the cause of the order of nature and the end (*Telos*) towards which that order tends. The definition of law that we endorsed in our chapter on law coincides with Plato's idea of the Good and Cicero's idea of natural laws governing human actions. Understanding this is not a matter of self-evident *a priori* knowledge but rather a matter of discovery by reason drawing inferences from experience. Plato presents the act of discovery through the Myth of the Cave in the Seventh book of the *Republic,* wherein one of the prisoners facing a wall in the cave with shadows passing across the wall is freed from his shackles. The shadows are what the prisoners took for knowledge and even made bets, using their memories, on which shadow would show up next. The freed prisoner turns around to discover that the shadows are caused by people carrying puppet-like artificial objects before a firelight and talking to each other, their voices echoing off the wall of the cave. The freed prisoner's efforts are painful and he is dazzled by the firelight. Slowly, he begins to recognize that the actions of these people accounts for what the prisoners see and hear. What they see and hear is what they allow them to see. Shall we call them the puppeteers? These people, we take it, are dwellers in the cave too. Their advantage over the prisoners is that they know that they are causing the shadows on and echoes off the wall of the cave. They are the makers of opinion in the cave, the "fashionistas." Otherwise they are no better than the prisoners in their knowledge of the causes of things. As the freed prisoner makes his way up the steep ascent and out of the cave, he finds that he is dazzled once again, this time by the daylight outside the cave. Slowly, he becomes accustomed to seeing natural things such as plants, animals, and men by their reflection in water and then the things themselves. After that he would learn more by watching the stars and planets by their light and that of the moon. Finally, he would look at the Sun and understand that it produces the seasons, the course of the year and controls everything in the perceivable part of the world. The sun in the perceivable part of the world corresponds to the Good in the intelligible part of the world. The Good is then understood to be not only the cause of the knowledge of things (i.e., knowing their nature and end), but the cause of the very existence of the things to be known.

But the myth of the cave has a dark side. When the freed prisoner returns to his place in the cave (for the cave is the place of the human condition), he can't see once again because of the darkness. The firelight and daylight hurt his eyes (implying that education and learning are painful); returning to the darkness of the cave was painful too. He could not see well enough to compete with his fellow prisoners in betting on the shadows. When he told them about what he had learned, they mocked him, saying that his eyesight had been ruined and that what he had learned was useless. If they could kill him, they would, because they understood that his knowledge called into question the artificiality of their lives.

Plato's point is that knowledge is pursued for its own sake, but there is a price to pay for it, the least of which is being accused of having one's head in the clouds and not having one's feet on the ground. Knowledge pursued for its own sake is the very opposite of the teaching of Machiavelli as is the Mosaic Code of morality that he mocks in the 11th and 18th chapters of *The Prince*. The Modernists have gone beyond Machiavelli's criticism of Moses. They hold him responsible, as the legendary author of the book of Genesis, for the unscientific idea that the world was created. But the worst villain and foe of Machiavelli's teaching is Jesus, not only for what Jesus taught which was the completion of the Mosaic Law, but especially for what Jesus was, namely, the Incarnate Word of God which perfects the Platonic logos making it no longer so utterly transcendent that it is beyond the world, but is at the same time immanent in the world.

A Warrior on the Premodern Side

The early courtiers of Modernity — from Machiavelli to Descartes to Locke to Rousseau to Voltaire to the *Illuminati* to Kant — did not have numbers of foes as celebrated as themselves. They were, after all, on the winning side of history. But every now and then someone emerged on the other side who was at or near their importance such as Donoso Cortès, Samuel Johnson, Jonathan Swift, Alexis De Toqueville and Joseph De Maistre. We will discuss briefly but one, Jonathan Swift, who saw clearly that a culture war existed and that it was between Pre-Modernity and Modernity. He describes that opposition differently in *The Battle of the Books* (1710) as between Ancient and Modern books, and he favors the Ancients over the Moderns. Modernity, according to Swift's satire, was not only a rash of theoretical errors but errors with grave moral consequences. They were mistakes contrary to truth and also contrary to good behavior. In other words, they were bad ideas. They were ideas that were *excessively* skeptical toward traditional religious and moral ideas and at the same time were excessively optimistic about human moral perfectibility, as we said in the chapter on religion. Furthermore these ideas attached themselves to the emerging science of Copernicus, Francis Bacon, Descartes, Galileo and Newton. Just as the New Science was challenging the old physics and astronomy, so too the new morality, a radical hedonism, and the new religion, a radical secularism, aimed at replacing traditional Western morality and religion. The success in the sciences was mistakenly and exuberantly transferred to morality and religion. This new morality and new religion received their extreme formulations later on in the work of such dark Enlightenment thinkers as Rousset de Missy, John Tolland, Julian de la Mettrie, Baron d'Holbach and the Marquis deSade and in an anonymous pamphlet entitled *Traitè de trois imposteurs* (1705?) which claimed that Moses, Jesus and Mohammed were imposters and frauds.

In the battle for supremacy between the Ancient books and those of the Moderns, Swift uses two inhabitants of the library where the battle is fought as representative of the habits of mind which belong to the opposing armies, namely those of the Bee and the Spider. The Spider "spins and spits wholly from himself and scorns to own any obligation or assistance from without. Then he displays to you his great skill in architecture and improvement in the mathematicks." On which the Bee comments "Erect your schemes with as much method as you please; yet if the materials be nothing but dirt, spun out of your own entrails (the guts of modern brains) the edifice will conclude at last in a cobweb: the duration of which, like that of other spiders' webs, may be imputed to their being forgotten, or neglected, or hid in a corner." Swift continues by having the Ancients declare:

> As for us Ancients, we are content with the Bee, to pretend to nothing of our own, beyond our wings and our voice: that is to say, our flights and our language; for the rest, whatever we have got, has been by infinite labor and search and ranging thro' every corner of nature: The difference is, that instead of dirt and poison we have rather chose to fill our lives with honey and wax, thus furnishing mankind with the two noblest of things, which are sweetness and light.

The Virtues and Benefits of Modern Thought

However much the sympathies of Brooklyn Existentialists lie with Swift and Premodern thought, critical common sense realism demands that they acknowledge and proclaim the virtues and benefits of modern thought (minus the isms) brought about by non-ideological science and technology, i.e., a science and technology aware of its limits. Not to do so would make them as stupid, foolish and doctrinaire as the ideological science and technology we discussed in chapters two and three. For example there is the modern doctrine of human and civil rights. In America it was the ground of a successful revolution and, in turn, to liberty, security and prosperity for its citizens. In France, however, its abuse led to a bloody civil revolution to terror, murder, and Napoleon's wars. In Russia, the "rights" revolution was a grand deception and the occasion for serfdom, insecurity, and poverty. As far as the Fascists and Nazis were concerned, there was not even the pretense of rights. But that rights doctrine would provide the hope and promise of liberty, security, and prosperity for Asia, Africa, and for Latin America. Indeed, in some parts of those continents, the hope has already been fulfilled and the promise kept. The folks there, as everywhere, must keep the tyrants and bullies under control and themselves in good moral order.

We may conclude, therefore, that the continuation of culture war in the crazy 20th Century did not stifle altogether the promise of imagination and civilization. But it drained some of the joy of savoring that promise, a promise that was quite marvelous when you consider the scientific discoveries and artistic creations that characterized the century. Consider too the technological products of that science and art which have made human life more comfortable, more expansive and more pleasing, despite two world wars. But the culture war has been out in the open for the last 40 years of the century to the dismay of the aggressors who continue to deny that they are involved in a culture war. These cultured aggressors perform their acts in masquerade. This is not to say that the campaigns are carried on only by Western insiders and only by stealth. Furthermore the culture war is not being waged only in the form of Western Moderns against the Premoderns, but it takes the form of the Postmoderns against the West itself, both Ancient and Modern.

Postmodern non-Westerners, who did not have a modern phase, have learned to recite the litany of the Western sins of patriarchism, colonialism, imperialism, racism, sexism, and homophobia. The masks, as critical common sense realists have discovered, were equality (all kinds), social justice, speeches and essays about freedom and multicultural originality. While excellence does exist everywhere, it doesn't always exist where the cultural elite says it does. Their rhetoric, which was mostly successful, took the means to a good and happy life to both an anomic (lawless) and absolute degree, thereby deliberately disordering them. What is finite cannot and should not be thought to be or to be made infinite

Before this culture war in and on the West reached its full and organized phase in the schools, the universities, the courts and law schools, the foundations, the museums, and the media, (all of which have "internalized" Gramscian Neo-Marxism), a host of technological marvels and beautiful things appeared and flourished in the first part of the 20th century, thanks again to the virtues of a free society. It is a good idea at this point to give a brief review of them. A new major art form came into existence, the motion picture, as did some splendid examples of modern (i.e., 20th Century) art in the *Art Nouveau* style which is found in the metro entrances in Paris (ca.1900), the Municipal House in Prague (1911) and the paintings of Gustav Klimt (1862-1918). Even more characteristic of modern 20th century art is that called *Art Deco* which received its name from the 1925 Paris Exhibition, *L'Exposition Internationale des Arts Décoratif et Industriels Modernes*. It began as an exclusive style for the *cognoscenti* and the rich, but then, fortunately, ordinary folks embraced it such that Art Deco was transformed into what is properly called "Depression Modern" and we call "Deco-Depression."

The Golden Gate Bridge (1937) in San Francisco, the Chrysler (1930) and Empire State (1931) buildings in New York City come to mind, as do the movie houses in that style such as the Radio City Music Hall (1932), also in New York City, and the Southtown Theater (1931) in Chicago. These movie houses, and others such as the former Roxy (1927) in the Art Nouveau style and the former Paramount (1926) in a Neo-Renaissance style, served as palaces for the simple pleasure of going to the movies for ordinary people, especially those making the subway trip to Manhattan from Brooklyn, the Bronx, and Queens, as well as the ferry ride from Staten Island. The people in Cicero took the Aurora & Elgin railway trip to Chicago. The Deco-Depression style even influenced American modern industrial buildings designed and constructed by the Austin Company of Cleveland.

In painting there were those such as *Girl in the Green Dress* (1929) of Tamara De Lempicka, and those of Erté such as *Beauty and the Beast* (1985).

In sculpture the statues of *Indian with a Bow* (1927) in Chicago's Grant Park by Ivan Mestrovic and *Prometheus* (1934) by Paul Manship (1886-1966) in Rockefeller Center, N.Y.C.

The splendor of Medieval stained glass was recaptured in the Art Nouveau style of Louis Comfort Tiffany. Like the Medieval originals, it was and is for the enjoyment and admiration of a wide spectrum of people. Art Nouveau and Deco-Depression styles in art objects could be found in every corner of the lives of ordinary people as in their daily use of Depression glass and Ronson lighters, making the Depression a little more tolerable. The same cannot be said for Modernist painting, sculpture, architecture, music and dance whose practitioners and exponents are at war with these modern styles and their popular appeal. Modernist and Postmodernist art require the more subtle and refined tastes of the cultural elite.

Until the First World War (1914-1918), eclectic 19th Century art continued into the 20th Century. Mark Twain's name for the last years of the 19th Century, "The Gilded Age," was equally applicable to the first of the 20th. This is evident in Art Nouveau and in the architecture of Richard Morris Hunt who designed "The Breakers" and "Marble House" in Newport, Rhode Island, as well as the Biltmore Estate in Asheville, North Carolina. We also find it in the many New York City buildings of Stanford White, including the homes he designed on 139th Street in Harlem, the old and lamented Pennsylvania Railroad Station and the arch in Washington Square Park. The Beaux Arts version of the Classical style of Grand Central Station designed and built by the firm of Reed and Stem, Warren and Whitmore is also Gilded Age, the Age that the class warriors among the elite like to call the Age of the Robber Barons. While we are touching on the subject of the Robber Barons, we assert with Brooklyn certitude that whatever their vices were, principally greed for wealth and lust for economic power, they could not match the murderous vices born of the major political ideologies of the 20th Century, which happened to be socialist in their economic ideas: Communism, Fascism, and Nazism. All three of these bad ideas emerged from the unsettled issues of World War I — in 1917, 1922, and 1933 respectively. They produced little or nothing of lasting artistic value. Social Realism was propaganda. At least people like the Vanderbilts, the Goulds, and the Fisks used some of their wealth for institutions of healing both for body and soul, such as hospitals, libraries, and museums. To compare their villainy to that of Hitler, Lenin, Trotsky, Stalin, Mao and Pol Pot whose thirst for justice and love of humanity produced institutions of torture, suffering, and violent death is bad quantitative thinking. While wars are terrible events to be avoided, they are not to be avoided at all costs; for example, in cases of self-defense, liberty and the protection of family and country against tyrants as those we just mentioned. Wars are also occasions for heroic virtue. Outside of those occasions, people of ordinary virtue would not rise to actions of extraordinary virtue in which heroism consists. Little good can be said for the invincibly ignorant smart-alecks who think that what we have just said is an advertisement for war. And little good can be said for those who have contempt for heroic virtue, interpreting it as an "ego trip."

The New Hedonism

The aggressive passions that were unleashed in the wars, massacres, and genocides in the crazy century were matched by the eruption of the erotic passions in a new hedonism — new because it was anointed by the pseudo-science of Freud, Kinsey, and the Frankfurters as well as the Dionysian philosophic affirmations of Friedrich Nietzsche, Michel Foucault, and Jacques Lacan. In Nietzsche and Foucault the erotic passions are wed to the aggressive passions giving birth to and in defining the human animal — reason and knowledge being the child of the passions. Sex is the way to know and knowing is a form of sex, both erupting in the will to power. Lacan is a revisionist Freudian who wishes to return to the "true" Freud as if the "true" Freud were no longer around and as if returning to the "true" Freud was something worth doing.

This new hedonism began in the 1920s, only to be curtailed briefly during the Great Depression of the '30s and the Second World War of the '40s. The curtailment was due to the necessity of sacrifice and self-restraint in those decades when suffering could not be avoided or escaped. The Australian philosopher, David Stove, spoke about and regretted the overturning of traditions in nearly every domain of human life as the promise of a "Great Reversal" and uses the title of one of Cole Porter's songs as its signifier: "Anything Goes" (1934). It refers not only to the "liberation" of the erotic passions but also to that of the aggressive passions as the century's madness so manifestly bears witness.

Great Discoveries and Inventions

On the positive side, there are the great discoveries and inventions that mark the century and have made human life more bearable and freer to pursue the specifically human activities of science, art, morality and religion which "the deep thinkers," as Thomas Sowell calls them, attribute to causes other than wonder, curiosity, intelligence, and leisure. In theoretical physics there is Einstein's theory of relativity on the cosmic level which makes corrections in Newtonian physics, the theory of indeterminacy of particle movement at the sub-atomic level, as proposed by such physicists as Neils Bohr and Werner Heisenberg. In chemistry we have Linus Pauling on chemical bonding which constitutes a new understanding of molecular structure. In biology we have the work of Watson, Crick and Wilkens, despite their dependence on and betrayal of Rosalind Franklin, on the double helical form of the DNA (Deoxyribonucleic acid) of living organisms.

On the practical side, there are the developments of indoor plumbing, the refrigerator, the gas (or electric) stove, electric lighting, electric tools, the washing machine, the dish washer, central heating, air conditioning, nuclear power for peaceful uses, and precision weaponry. For transportation, communication, and entertainment, there are the developments of the motor car, the airplane, ships propelled by power fuels, the radio, the phonograph, the moving picture, the television, the telephone, radar, sonar and their electronic spinoffs (e.g. CDs and DVDs). There were the inventions of solid state electronics, the microprocessor, the transistor, the mini computer, which among their many uses, made possible current medical technology including CAT scans, MRIs, and robotics. The development of illness-curing and life-saving drugs have made the old Dupont advertising slogan — "Better lining through chemistry" — an evident fact.

Technological developments in sports, as with much of technology, are ambiguous. At their best, sports promote health and strength and above all are occasions for excellence of judgment and courage, as Aristotle said in the *Nicomachean Ethics*. We have already mentioned their descent into show biz which is what leads us to call their development ambiguous. As regards technology, the ambiguity resides in its abuse and the dependence it causes.

Mentioning some of these technologies, we are struck by the fact that in a limited sense, they have conquered space, time, and environment. They have done this at affordable cost to consumers. Furthermore, at the risk of calling down on our heads the wrath of the mindlessly righteous, for what they would regard as our justification for colonialism, we can say that these technologies have made life in colonial Africa and Asia during the first part of the crazy century not only more tolerable but even more enjoyable for their populations. The technologies used for farming and mining come to mind, as do those of transportation and communication. It was a life that the independence movements did not sustain, at least in Africa. The instances are many, but we will mention but one — The Zimbabwe of today. India, of course, has faired better than Africa and China in this regard. China, despite economic success, still needs political freedom. Places like Hong Kong and Singapore took the technology and ran with it, shall we say, for a touchdown.

In the West, the geometric forms of the Trylon and Perisphere, the emblem of the New York 1939 World's Fair, signified, for parts of the Americas and Europe, the promise of art and technology for the "World of Tomorrow."

This was the very year World War II began in Europe and dampened for a while the optimism of the Fair.

Modernist Painting and Other Modernist Arts

In the scientific and technological orders, the movement and direction is, with few exceptions, progressive. Theories and inventions build on one another. They are exercises in objectivity, that is, they are public in character and in use. They are accessible to everyone who attends to them. In the arts of the 20th century, however, the movement and direction was toward ever greater degrees of abstraction and subjectivity, indeed, subjectivism. Most, not all, of the "isms" of 20th century art are instances of this general fact: Expressionism, Abstract Expressionism, Fauvism, Dadaism, Futurism, Surrealism, Purism, Minimalism and Hyper-Realism are some of the names for the abstractions from nature to the ego of the artist. Famous names come to mind: Picasso, Duchamp, Mondrian, Braque, Chagall, Matisse, Nolde, Kandinsky, Marc, Klee, Pollack, Rothko, Motherwell, Lichtenstein, Johns, and Warhol among painters; Brancusi, Matisse, and Calder among sculptors; Gehry, Johnson, and Piano among architects. Even the Marxist revolutionary paintings of Kalo, Rivera, and Orozco are not exceptions to the trend. The intentions of Cubism and Abstractionism both are and are not. They are in that they abstract from the way things look in nature; they are not in that their aim is to disclose the "essence" of things in a kind of super Platonism. The aim, as guru art critic, Clement Greenberg put it, was to get close to or at the essence of things.

There were other 20th century artists who did not move in that direction at all, but rather toward some forms of realism, such as the romantic realism of Andrew Wyeth, the urban depression realism of Edward Hopper, and the rural regional realism of Grant Wood and Thomas Hart Benton. These American artists were, in fact, explicitly antimodernist.

In their attempt to portray the geometric shape of things in a kind of Retro-pythagoreanism or as in Abstractionism, the pure form of things, Modernist painters and sculptors were trying to separate the idea or form of a thing from its matter. In poetry the reverse occurred. Modernist poets promoted freedom from verse and versification. This was their desire to have content without form. The movement in the writing of novels was toward the psychological, normal or abnormal, as the case may be. Stream of consciousness in Marcel Proust and free-floating imagination and word-play in James Joyce are prominent examples. Architecture does not so easily lend itself to subjectivism because of the public meaning and use of buildings. This did not stop architects such as Le Corbusier from trying, when stressing the purely spiritual aspect of building such that architecture must appear as a "pure creation of the spirit." It did not stop Philip Johnson when promoting the absence of "retrograde" adornment in the International Style (Bauhaus) or the collapsing-upon-itself look of the Deconstructionist style.

The distortion or abstraction of shapes in sculpture may be interesting but they are still distortions or abstractions and, therefore, projections of ideas from the sculptor's mind as those from the minds of Brancusi, Matisse, Giacometti, Henry Moore, or Maya Lin. But then there is the Monumental realism of Frederick Hart whose sculptures are traditional and exhibit triumph, defeat, and the forbidden (by the Art Establishment) sense of magnificence.

"Form Follows Function"

Since we are talking about shapes, we should mention an artistic slogan of the 20th century used mainly by designers of cars and furniture and especially by some architects: "Form follows function." The first thing to be said about it is that "form" means shape and not "form" in the Platonic and Aristotelian sense, i.e., as the spirit or essence of a thing. Consequently teleology turns up in the slogan in that the function of a thing or object is that for the sake of which it exists, i.e., what the thing is supposed to be. Postmodernist architects such as Robert Venturi reject the slogan. It does, after all, have the quality of restricting or inhibiting the free play of shapes.

If "anything goes," then there are no limits to ideas, imagination, or action. The self expands and perpetuates itself because there can be no limitations placed on it by the natural, moral, or esthetic orders. Given its enthusiasm, the religious domain, to no surprise, was not immune. For example, the Catholic Church had its *aggiornamento* through the desires of the liberal members of its clergy at the Second Vatican Council (1962-1965). The Council was intended to bring the Church up to date and to come to terms with Modernity. New is good, and modern is good. Only the benighted traditionalists could quarrel with that. Ironically, it was the "backward" Catholic Church that led the revolutionary charge of the '60s.

Some of the consequences, both intended and unintended, were a secularization of and alienation from the Church's tradition, its mystery, its art and its liturgy. The quest for religious liberty and a more ecumenical spirit, just and worthy goals, did not escape the siren call of "anything goes."

"Understanding" Modernist Art

Returning to Modernist art, we can and do say that all its "isms" are more than a clue to understanding it and why it was a bad idea. Viewers had to be "instructed" and persuaded as to the meaning and passion of Modernist art. Esthetics was no longer about beauty and skillful craft although there is no doubt that Modernist artists had eyes for beauty and could make things well. Beauty and craft, however, were not the point. Individual expression, creativity, reversal, and shock were. Modernist art was an exercise in *épater le bourgeoisie*, i.e., an elitist sticking it to the folks. It is "idea" art, theoretical art, revolutionary art, theatre-of-ideas art. It is, to paraphrase Tom Wolfe, the painted idea, but our remarks are not limited to painting. Modernist art is not a case of the idea made flesh, but it is an instance of the Gnostic rejection of matter, or as the opposite abstraction has it, the materialist rejection of form. In both cases we find the esoteric aspect of Gnosticism, namely the secret knowledge shared only by the insiders. Thus we have painters painting for painters and for critics, architects building for architects, composers composing for composers, poets writing for poets. It is art reduced to pure idea, showing that these artists and supporting critics could not free themselves from the snares of their own esthetic delinquencies. It also shows the everlasting discontent of the *pure* intellectual. Beauty is not enough. These artists believe that they must show that beauty and order are rooted in ugliness and disorder. It is as if beauty were an affront to their originality. Blinded by their obsession with originality, they fail to understand that originality does not count, if the work of art possesses no value beyond originality, i.e., if it is not beautiful, instructive or ennobling.

It should come as no surprise then that the art establishment provided forums for exercises by such artists in the debasement of beauty. One was at New York's Whitney Museum in an exhibit called "Abject Art" in 1993. Another took place in London in 1997 in an exhibit by young British artists called "Sensation." Charles Saatchi, a collector of and publicist for Modernist art, provided the pieces for the exhibition. Reports were that the exhibit was popular. To our dismay, when the exhibit came to the United States in 1999, it was housed in Brooklyn at the Brooklyn Museum where viewers were treated to among other "masterpieces," a work by Chris Ofili called the Holy Virgin Mary. It depicted a black Madonna decorated with elephant dung and encircled by collaged images of genitalia taken from pornographic magazines. Following public disapproval, taxpayer funding for the exhibit was suspended until Judge Nina Gershon ruled that it be restored. The restoration for the funding of the exhibit was in true elitist fashion.

Art and Some Philosophers

They take their cue from a passage in Friedrick Nietzsche's *Birth of Tragedy* (1872). That some of them did not read Nietzsche is not at issue. His teaching was already in the intellectual climate of the 20th century. In the third chapter, Nietzsche relates the following:

> *An old legend has it that King Midas hunted a long time in the woods for the wise Silenus, companion of Dionysios, without being able to catch him. When he had finally caught him, the king asked him what he considered man's greatest good. The daemon remained sullen and uncommunicative until finally, forced by the king, he broke into a shrill laugh and spoke: 'Ephemeral wretch, begotten by accident and toil, why do you force me to tell you what it would be your greatest boon not to hear? What would be best for you is quite beyond your reach: not to have been born, not to be, to be nothing. But the second best is to die soon.*

How's that for an enchanting idea! With it Nietzsche captures all other ideas, good and bad, in that one. He wasn't yet insane when he wrote that. He is not just talking about suicide, but about not being at all, and not only for King Midas, but for everything and everyone. Nietzsche was no two-bit college professor atheist with a s…eating grin on his face, but one who thinks it tragic that God does not exist. For him, not-to-be is better than to be in a kind of dramatic and romantic atheism. It is non-being and death that are good and desirable. Now, that's reversal!

Like this romantic atheism, the subjectivism of Modernist art, when it exists not only for self-gratification, but also for public consumption, has to be justified, i.e., reasons must be given and accepted as to why its products should be considered art. In the case of Romantic atheism, the reasons given are the absurdity and horror of existence. The flight from objectivity is short.

A Pragmatist philosopher like John Dewey, for another example, must appeal to the practicality and usefulness of art in an enlightened democracy. Thus art is a function of the political. Of course, for the Marxists, art must be politicized. It must promote social and economic equality. It cannot and ought not be dissociated from the world of politics, according to Theodor Adorno and Walter Benjamin. Both they and French Existentialist, Jean Paul Sartre, maintain that art must be *committed*, where commitment means bringing about the socialist revolution by any means possible and all means necessary. Beauty gets lost or is a distraction. On the other hand, Elaine Scarry asserts that beauty is not a distraction from social justice, but rather is preparation for it. For Martin Heidegger, however, the crucial relationship for beauty is not political but *ontological*. It is the relationship of beauty to truth, that is to say, that truth is a disclosure of reality and beauty is one way in which that disclosure occurs. Umberto Eco, although a Postmodernist in tendency, calls himself a Thomist, partly in jest, because he is something of a joker. Yet he gives a straightforward account of the Medieval distinction and the connection between beauty and goodness. This means that while beauty is one of the good things, it is through beauty, i.e., through the pleasing quality of things beheld, that one recognizes their goodness, i.e., their desirability which awakens in the viewer or listener the desire to enter into a mystical communion with them.

Pop Art

The trickster in Eco is also found in the art called "Op" and "Pop." What we have here is parody. "Op" and "Pop" are neither optical nor popular. True op and pop art are found in the movies, the songs of Cole Porter and Rogers and Hart, the dancing of Fred Astaire, the choreography of Busby Berkely, the singing of Frank Sinatra and the paintings of Maxfield Parrish, Norman Rockwell and Frank Frazetta, scorned by the Art Establishment "Community" as mere "illustrations."

While we are talking this way about true Pop art, we should say a word or two about true mobile art; and it's not going to be about Alexander Calder's "mobiles" which didn't move that much but did see some use as patterns for crib toys. We're talking about the 1942 Indian motorcycle, Gordon Buehrig's 1937 Cord automobile and 1932 Duesenberg SJ, most Ferraris and the Teutels' Orange County Choppers, none of which needs arcane explanations or "gentle" persuasion to be considered mobile art.

In order to grasp the "put on" feature of establishment "Pop" and "Op," we must also grasp the Postmodernist talk about the "meaning" of art. While Postmodernism is a denial of the rationalism of the Enlightenment, it is as the same time, an affirmation of the deepest level of the Enlightenment, i.e., of the Radical Enlightenment of Lamettrie, d'Holbach, and de Sade. The deepest level is that of the unfettered will to do anything at all as in "anything goes." What we said about the "isms" at the beginning and the middle of the 20th century applies to beauty and craft. They have no meaning or purpose other than to restrict the artist. Beauty and craft do not count. Expressiveness, novelty, originality and the "Put on" do; the last particularly in the work of Andy Warhol, whose groupies felt safe from his mocking of the bourgeoisie. For what is more beautiful, i.e., pleasing to the Modernist and Postmodernist mind, than to shock and revile the bourgeoisie, whose own pleasure consists in their complicity in being deceived. For they look at, admire, praise and buy the "artwork."

Modernist Music

Music composers and music critics kept pace with the *Zeitgeist* by making war on melody, rhythm, harmony, counterpoint, and finally on the sound of music itself. Frankfurters had a hand in this too in the person of Theodor Adorno who wrote an apologetic for Modernist music in his *Philosophy of Modern Music* (1949). Modernist music is "idea" music in that the affirmation of cacophony had to be justified by the usual bad ideas couched in the sophistry about originality. The reversals move from tonality to dissonance to atonality found in the works of Bartok, Stravinsky, Schoenberg, Berg and Cage. The fact that music lovers preferred to listen to Bach, Vivaldi, Mozart, Beethoven, Tchaikovsky, Johann Strauss, Verdi and Puccini cuts no ice with the revolutionaries, who insisted on instructing those music lovers on their lack of openness to the profound things that Modernist music was saying. Whatever it was saying, Modernist music was not making beautiful sound. We mention only parenthetically the Modernist influence of Diaghilev whose treatment of graceful bodily movement, that is, dance, coincided with the revolution in music.

The best example we can give of the descent of music into silence is John Cage's "composition" *Four Minutes, Thirty-Three Seconds*. A musician (we suppose) enters the stage, sits at the piano for the four minutes and thirty-three seconds of the masterpiece's title, takes sips of water from a glass, turns some pages which look like music sheets, then bows and leaves. Virtuosity through mimicry and yet no interesting paradox of the sounds of silence here, just silence. To confirm how such a happening as this can be considered "great art," indeed a masterpiece, just read *The Wall Street Journal's* music critic, Peter Gutman's recent panegyric (*Wall Street Journal*, 3/24-25/07, p. P18).

It is not hard to recognize whose bad idea is worse: Cage's idea of non-musical music or the critic's idea that it is a masterpiece which has "philosophical import" and opens "as wide a window to eternity as any venerable favorite by Bach, Beethoven or Mozart." The only philosophical import the piece has is that it is empty nonsense, while the critic's judgment of it is full nonsense. The "masterpiece" does not open a window to eternity but to the void. The bad idea of conceiving and promoting the piece as a masterpiece is worse. For without the endorsement of the critic and the music establishment, music lovers would ignore the piece as merely another exercise in deception (the "put on") by the elitists. This stuff transcends Marshall McCluhan's medium being the message. But McCluhan did get it right about Modernist Art when he suggested that it is the paint, not the painting; it's the sound not the music; it's the reporter not the story; it's the words not the sense; it's the abstraction of either the form without the content or the content without the form. Bad ideas — all!

Modernist Architecture

Robert Venturi, architect, writer, and Postmodernist rightly castigates the puritanically moral language of the Modernists who can, as he says, no longer intimidate architects. He is referring to Walter Gropius, to the Bauhaus School in general and to the "spiritual" Le Corbusier. Bauhaus was as much a school of philosophy as it was of architecture. According to it, buildings had to be free of ornamentation. Arches, crown moldings, keystones, domes, and steeples were an affront to the principle "less is more." Housing for the proletariat had to be *"Wohnmachinen"* (living machines). Designs had to be flat, sharp, and functional. No *Art Nouveau* or *Art Deco* for the plebs whose tastes were spoiled by buildings like the movie theaters of the '30s. As in painting, so too in architecture, deontological flatness is the idea, not beauty. Bauhaus buildings possess shape but not form and, therefore, are devoid of spirit. They mock elegant simplicity.

Shape follows function, especially in poured or reinforced concrete, and in the glass and metal boxes like the Lever and Seagrams building in N.Y.C. Yet Lever and Seagram have some architectural character compared to what Gropius proposed for poor people. For them, multi-storied public housing in city areas of high density population, are the ticket such as the Fort Greene Houses in Brooklyn and the Robert Taylor Homes in Chicago — warehouses of crime and violence. It appears that the bad ideas of the architectural revolution end in bathetic conformity and sometimes in the quiet desperation of those who bear the burden of those ideas.

Venturi finds that less is more boring and tries to jettison the rule that shape follows function. He says in *Complexity and Contradiction in Architecture (1966):*

I like elements which are hybrid rather than 'pure,' compromising rather than 'clean,' distorted rather than 'straightforward,' ambiguous rather than 'articulated,' perverse as well as impersonal, boring as well as interesting, conventional rather than 'designed,' accommodating [including] rather than excluding, redundant rather than 'simple,' vestigial as well as 'innovating,' inconsistent and equivocal rather than direct and clear. I am for messy vitality over obvious unity. I include the non sequitur and proclaim the duality.

In other words, an architecture of complexity, contradiction, disharmony, disorder, disunity and the splendor of foolishness!

Although he doesn't get all his oppositions correctly matched, we do get the idea. If he understood contradiction, he'd realize that he can't have contradiction in architecture which amounts to an absolute denial of what anyone affirms. Contrariety, yes; contradiction, no. Contrariety goes with complexity, not contradiction. You can say, for example, that Zebras are black and white, but you can't say that Zebras *are* black and white and *are not* black and white at the same time. Then he speaks of "obvious" unity. Is his quarrel with obvious unity rather than unity? He does not address the important and true distinction he has made. A thing may possess unity and yet its unity may not be obvious. For example, as in *E Pluribus Unum*. Despite his quibbles, what he says is an excellent manifesto of Postmodernism. Michel Foucault would add to what Venturi has said (and we don't believe Venturi would say it) by suggesting that we must look into the corners and cracks of this Postmodernist consciousness of art and beauty so as to normalize and proclaim its deviancy.

Return of the Premodern

The differences between Modernism and Postmodernism seem to be a family quarrel among artists and critics, while other artists and philosophers have returned to a Premodern consciousness, something that the philosopher, Hegel, believed could not and should not be done given his view of the inevitable and linear progress of history. As the cliché says, "You can't turn back the clock." The culture of the past is just a memory. Yet this Premodern consciousness is found in the later poems and criticism of T.S. Eliot, the sculpture of Alexander Stoddart and Frederick Hart, the philosophies of Martin Heidegger and Etienne Gilson, the novels and stories of Flannery O'Connor, ("that hillbilly Thomist"), the paintings of Brooklyn by Brooklynite, Nicholas Evans Cato, and the popular Palladian style that can be seen in houses and storefronts all over America in the 21st Century (which are not just parodies of that style as the Postmodernists claim). It is a turn toward what delights the eye, ear, heart and mind on the part of the observer and craft on the part of the artist. While this consciousness is aware of the lures, enticements, and deceptions of beauty, it does not regard beauty, as Nietzscheans do, as a mask for the absurdities and terrors of human life. Beauty is not the picture of Dorian Gray. Nor does it kill us as it was said to have done to a great fabled ape by the name of Kong.

Photography and the Movies

Which brings us to photography and the movies! The second was dependent on the first, which was invented in the 19th Century. The photos done by Matthew Brady are an early form. But those two arts had an amicable separation in 20th Century such that, among other things, the artist of the photograph is the photographer, whereas the principal artist of the motion picture is the director commanding the cinematographer, the screenwriter, the editor, and the actors. It is curious but true that artists of the early 20th Century believed that they had to distance themselves from the photographic image in order to affirm originality and individuality. Photography is its own separate art. It is not true that the photograph displays things as they exist in nature or as in a mirror. As in all art, the depiction is not only of the qualities of the beheld but also for the eye of the beholder. To say this in another way, the artists, their subjects and their beholders commune in the work of art. The photograph is not a literal depiction, if literal means a passive reflection of nature. Photographers capture the subject in a specific moment of space and time, framing and composing the subject in an order in which the artists are participating. When that framing and composition are done well (according to proportion, mood, integrity and harmony) we have photographs like those of Alfred Stieglitz, Edward Steichen, Cartier Bresson, Margaret Bourke White, Ansel Adam and Richard Avedon whose works combine originality, beauty, and craft which elicit and receive attention and admiration. On the other hand, the sado-masochistic photographs of Robert Maplethorpe exhibit skill but not art. Subject matter as well as skill or form is required for a work to pass as a work of art.

The technology of the motion picture builds on the technology of the photograph. In portraying dramatic action, the motion picture is on film while the stage play is live, but the motion picture expands exponentially the rendering of dramatic action. But both should be experienced in darkened theatres. The small screen of the television does diminish the power of the experience of movies. TV, however, is its own art form borrowing from vaudeville, the movies and radio. The chief artists of TV are the writers and the producers. Despite its virtues, TV seems to have become the true opiate of the people.

To succeed as works of art, movies must entertain and delight, teach, edify, or ennoble, but must not disgust, or bore as in the pornography of shock, violence, and "special effects." When they teach, they cannot be preachy, propagandistic or moralistic. The parts — the script, the development of character, the editing, the acting, the music (if there is music), the montage, and above all, the cinematography — must unite in dialectical interplay of intelligence and feeling. The director, through his cinematic imagination, is the artist who fashions the union. Attempts at deliberate disorder, gratuitous violence, and self-conscious novelty, as in the Postmodern "films" of director Quentin Tarantino, despite his talents, seem to be directed toward "filmworms," i.e., devotees whose lives are constituted by "films." So too does the "footnoting" whereby later films refer to earlier ones, as when a scene in *Rocky (1976)* refers to a scene in *On the Waterfront* (1954). The portrayal of boredom in *La Notte* (1961) by Michelangelo Antonioni and of "ambiguity" in Alain Resnais' *Last Year at Marienbad (1961)* are just that, boring and ambiguous. We should not forget that absolute ambiguity is a Postmodern virtue. Sometimes the reach for novelty is beyond grasp of the artist.

Originality with craft, however, was often achieved by such directors and actors as Afred Hitchcock, Charlie Chaplin, the Marx Brothers, Buster Keaton, Orson Welles, Sergei Eisenstein, Mack Sennet, Laurel and Hardy, D.W. Griffith, Frank Capra, John Huston, Billy Wilder, John Ford, Akira Kurosawa, Ingmar Bergman, Federico Fellini, Satyajit Ray, Francois Truffault and Lina Wertmuëller. Actors are mixed in with the directors here, because some actors were themselves, "the show" through their improvisations.

As the characteristic art form of the 20th Century, the motion picture can and does, through its technology, present other art forms of the visual and aural kind. It can tell, besides its own stories, through the kindred medium of television, the story of painting, sculpture, architecture, and the sound of music. It does more than what opera was supposed to do, unite drama and music. It must tell stories. As the course of history is dramatic and not linear, so too the movies must be dramatic. It is a bad Postmodernist idea that stories, because they are little unities, cannot and must not be told. Postmodernists say that life and history are open-ended, beginning in chaos and ending in chaos — ideas for which these geniuses have not the slightest evidence. For them, stories cannot be but open-ended.

Hooray for openness!

The motion picture is not only the characteristic art form of the 20th century, but is also its popular art as well. When successful, it possesses relationships with beauty, truth and goodness as any other art, regardless of its time and place, with its ability to please perception because it possesses integrity, harmony, and splendor of form; for being pleasing to perception is what beauty means, while integrity, harmony, and splendor of form are in what a beautiful thing consists. And you heard that from the Brooklyn stoops.

EPILOGUE

The *Four Horsemen* from the book of the *Apocalypse* (a.k.a. *Revelation, Ch.6, vs.6*), is an apt denomination for those "idea" men who brought aggression (the White Horse), war (the Red Horse), famine (the Black Horse) and pestilence (the Pale Horse), into the world of ideas in the 20th and 21st centuries. The Apocalyptic jockeys are Marx, Darwin, Freud and Nietzsche who can change horses whenever they need to. Their ideas were the most influential in deforming the culture of the 20th century. The errant missionary effort was carried out by disciples as eager and as devoted as the early Christian missionaries. Each of the idea men proposed doctrines which were in themselves total explanations of reality but which in some ways complemented one another. The Frankfurt school of "critical thought" arranged a happy marriage between Freud and Marx. Freud and Nietzsche shared the Darwinian drive and thrust from randomness to order, while Darwin's idea of natural selection shared the thrust and drive of Freud's and Nietzsche's Dionysian Eros.

All four were materialists. Those of an ecumenical cast of mind about Darwinism and religion, Christianity in particular, either ignore or are unaware of what Darwin wrote in his unexpurgated autobiography about his scientific studies.

> *Thus disbelief crept over me at a very slow rate, but was at last complete. The rate was so slow that I felt no distress, and have never doubted even for a single moment that my conclusion was correct. I can indeed hardly see how anyone ought to wish Christianity to be true; for if so, the plain language of the text seems to show that the men who do not believe, and this would include my Father, Brother, and almost all my best friends, will be everlastingly punished. And this is a damnable doctrine (Darwin, p. 87).*

It seems that Darwin's religious conversion took place at a slow imperceptible rate to a new stage in just the way he described the evolution of species: descent with modification from a common ancestor.

Richard Dawkins in his recent book on atheism gets it right. To be a Darwinian in evolutionary theory is to be an atheist. You don't, however, have to be a Darwinian to be an atheist. Dawkins gets it right and the mush head ecumenists don't.

All four were determinists. They denied free human choice. Marx believed that economic and social forces compelled human beings to act as they do. Freud believed that the Id (libido or lust) compelled them to act as they do. For Nietzsche people are driven by irrational forces beyond their control, and for Darwinians it is the impersonal force of natural selection. The Neo-Darwinian twist on that is that our genes compel us to do what we do. The Behaviorists who had a special influence on psychology and education professors offered a variant of the Marxist version of determinism. They believe that human beings are the products or sum total of their environmental conditioning; they have no freedom, that is, no deliberate choice among alternatives offered by nature and society; no responsibility for those actions that produce civilization. According to these deep thinkers, human beings do not initiate action in the world through reason and choice, but they are said to be in the grip of some force or another, be it something other than themselves such as economic conditions, or the environment, or some part of themselves, other than reason and choice, such as unconscious irrational forces or their genes struggling to dominate the gene pool. Reason and choice are not what define human beings as human beings, but they are derivatives or functions of these other forces which, according to the deep thinkers, are what truly define human beings. For the Darwinian deep thinker, this means that the differences between a one-celled organism and a human beings are *not* differences in kind (qualitative) but only differences of degree (quantitative), differences of more or less. An amoeba's life is simply less than a man's but not of a different quality. Reason and choice happen to exist only along a continuum of small quantitative changes.

To affirm reason, freedom, and individual responsibility against determinism is not, however, to claim that they are unconditioned. Reason and choice are not compelled or determined but they are influenced and conditioned by such things as nature, history, environment, habit, desire, and fear. Freedom of choice is not absolute or unconditional, as the French-y Existentialist, Jean-Paul Sartre, claims. This idea of freedom has had its greatest resonance in the rhetoric of abortion. Unfortunately, when careless semi-educated people speak of Existentialism, it is Sartre's Existentialism and his faulty idea of freedom that they have in mind. There are other Existentialist philosophers whose account of freedom is more sound. For example, the Italian Existentialist, Nicola Abbagnano, conceives of freedom in the negative sense as the absence of compulsion; however, he conceives of it primarily in the positive sense as the possibility of choice among alternatives offered by nature and history. Then there is Brooklyn Existentialism which uses as its metaphor for freedom the idea of "playing the hand you are dealt" and reflects Abbagnano's conception. The limits on freedom are the cards you are dealt by nature, history, and environment and the other aforementioned limits.

We join here this sound idea of freedom with the complementary idea of freedom we discussed in our chapter on education, in particular, the section on liberal education. There we argued that liberal education consists in the study of those disciplines which are studied for their own sake and not out of necessity or utility. Such study is intended to form persons capable of responsible self-determination. This means that a person who is free is master over his opinions and his passions and, of course, is not the slave of others or their opinions and passions. The person who is free exists for his own sake. He is his own man. She is her own woman. And this is without arrogance but rather with that sense of finitude which is a defining note of Existentialism.

In the course of our discussion we have tried to show that the ideas of the influential four have produced aggression, famine, pestilence in and war on Premodern ideas, mostly the good ones, good because they are true, because they are desirable, or because they are ennobling. Reason, choice and responsibility are the distinctive human characteristics. These are the characteristics uncovered both by critical common sense and by critical self-consciousness. They are not the products of passion, either erotic or aggressive. They are not the smoke given off by "socio-economic" conditions. Nor are they undifferentiated stages in the evolutionary process. And they are surely not fictions by which we keep the absurdity and horror of nature at bay. Saying that they are is the way the so-called masters of suspicion and their disciples poisoned and intended to poison those distinctive human characteristics.

Rather, critical common sense realism can and does say that the passions are the result of human recognition of a thing which as an act of reason permits us to desire, fear, hate, and choose or reject it.

The Marxist, Freudian, Darwinian, and Nietzschean theories themselves are products of reason and not the passions, and in being such, confirm the primacy of reason. Bad theories as well as good theories are the products of reason. Deliberate bad theories include the desire to deceive, to dominate others' minds. This is just another verification of the limits of reason. But it is still reason that pronounces on and presents things to the passions and the will for decision.

The big four of the 20th Century have not been the only ones to produce the bad ideas of our time. We mentioned John Dewey and William Heard Kilpatrick whose bright ideas, proposed, we must assume, with the best of intentions, played a part in the decline of American education. Margaret Mead engaged in the deception about free innocent sex without guilt, jealousy and the other usual consequences of promiscuity. Alfred Kinsey too had his say about sex which was equally deceitful but nevertheless was profoundly influential. The school of Frankfurt had its mostly "uncritical" dialectics on politics, sex, and art. It had its greatest sway not as much in Europe as in the USA. The Humanistic psychologists, such as Carl Rogers, dehumanized people through their instructions to let go of the emotions, to let, as they said, "everything hang out" on the supposition that emotional restraint is the cause of mental disorder.

In the physical sciences, which have produced mostly good ideas, in that knowledge is the result, one problem has been the disregard for the limits of science, especially in the form of scientism, i.e., science as religion and bad philosophy (materialism).

Another problem has been the fraudulent claims made in behalf of unproven or half-proven theories, as is the case with Ernst Haeckel, a Darwinian true believer.

Finally, the last problem has been to assert atheism on the basis of "scientific" theories or problems. Here we call into question the "faith" of scientists who claim that the complexity and diversity of nature spring from random play of lifeless material particles, i.e., from an absolute chaos which, like formless matter, does not exist and has never been experienced by anyone, nor could it be. If it is believed as a matter of inference, then that is a bad inference. Disorder, a falling apart of order, does occur, and we do experience it and often. But disorder is not absolute chaos. It is dependent on order for its existence and for the possibility of understanding it.

Here Brooklyn Existentialism as critical common sense realism, offers a version of Pascal's "Wager" on whether God exists or not and the consequences of wagering on one assertion or the other. The choices are that nature, in all its complexity and diversity sprang from an absolute chaos or it was produced by an intelligent cause. Which choice is the better example of *blind* faith? The gang on the stoop and everybody else would like to know.

Speaking of blind faith, we have suggested in the chapter on religion that such a faith is one of the bad ideas in that domain. Another is believing a doctrine or a practice that is contrary to nature and reason, such as ritual murder and suicide. Then there are such gods as would command such practices, or a god who would condemn to perdition anyone who does not have free choice and personal responsibility. Bad ideas!

Then there is the bad idea of following a false Messiah such as Jim Jones, Marxist and preacher. How do you tell a false Messiah from a true one? By what that Messiah says, does, and teaches others to do! Jesus holds up rather well in this regard.

A religion founded on *schmaltz, i.e.,* a religion of sweet thoughts and smarmy feelings is not a religion worthy of the name. Here we paraphrase the monk, Zossima, a character in Dostoyevsky's *The Brothers Karamazov* (1880) as regards sweet religious feelings. "[Religion] in action is a harsh and dreadful thing compared to [religion] in dreams."

As far as the bad ideas in the law are concerned, we saw that they were both theoretical and practical. The bad theoretical ones were those concerning the concept of law itself. To think that law is essentially force and the will of the ruler (or rulers) is not to think about law. Add to this that the "scientific" concept of law has little or nothing to do with the concept of justice and you have thinking that has lost its way or has a vested interest, as law professors and lawyers have a tendency to have. We have this on the highest authority: Plato, Jesus, and Shakespeare. For these bad ideas we have such predecessors as Marx, as Thomas Hobbes and John Austin to thank and such 20th Century positivists as Hans Kelsen. It is no accident, then, that the rule of law has become in great part the rule of lawyers. With the psychologists controlling what we say, there are the lawyers controlling what we do.

Then there is the theory that the law is connected to a natural rights doctrine which has indeed had some merit, namely as the basis of civil rights for citizens whom the law did not protect. But, as we have seen, the doctrine of rights is intoxicating. It has been extended to protect animals and trees, to protect criminals, to protect the right to abort one's own offspring, to protect terrorists as having the same rights as citizens, to protect a right to seditious speech and action (such as flag burning), to protect pornography as speech, to protect a right to same sex marriage, to protect the right of privacy for children against the duties and responsibility of parents. Who knows where else the doctrine of rights will extend? For it is a doctrine easily and quickly learned, especially in an atmosphere of victimization where whole classes of people who believe or are told to believe that they are victims of something. That some of them are is a truism.

No major area of human activity was left untouched by bad ideas and the culture war where those bad ideas were weapons of incremental destruction. The separation of justice from law had its counterpart in the separation of beauty from art in the field of creativity. Concern for beauty and craft in the minds of ideological artists and critics was regarded as naïve and jejune. Originality and novelty were the points of reference for Modernist art. Our distinction between Modern art and Modernist art refutes the accusation that to stand for beauty is to stand against originality. Beauty, moreover, is not "in the eye of the beholder" as that worn out cliché and bad idea says it, if the cliché means that beauty is subjective. It is not so that everyone has his own idea of beauty, which is in part what subjective means. Rather everyone has the same idea of beauty. Beauty means that which is pleasing to perception. When anyone says that someone or something is beautiful, that is what they mean. People *may* differ as to what *things* they call beautiful, but their idea of beauty is the same. And if they differ, they don't differ that much. Why else do we have museums which contain beautiful works of art from many and various cultures? Why else do we have beauty contests where women of various races and ethnicities compete equally? We should not repeat that mush that someone is beautiful on the inside, unless one means that the someone has good character. Good character is not the same as beauty. The only sense in which the assertion "beauty is in the eye of the beholder" is true is in the sense that anything visible is experienced by means of the eyes.

The 20th Century has produced many works of great beauty in painting, sculpture, music and architecture, and it has done so despite the dogmas of Modernism shared by some, but not all, artists, critics and art dealers. Nevertheless the art establishment is among that some. For themselves and for others, the uninitiated, they get to say what art is and what it is not. Establishment architecture such as Bauhaus could not last because its simplicity was ugly and boring and not elegant. As architect, Robert Venturi, paraphrasing the Bauhaus slogan, "less is more," said: "less is more boring."

Technology and the great inventions of the 20ᵗʰ and 21ˢᵗ centuries are not in themselves spoiled or poisoned by their abuse and our dependence on them. Nearly every aspect of human life has been expanded and improved through that technology and these inventions. The list of those aspects is too long and too well known to mention again. We did mention some already in our chapter on technology. The one domain where technology is a mixed blessing is that of politics, where pushing people around has been made easier.

The culture war fought with and against bad ideas has had two phases. The first is the battle of the Modern world against the Premodern world (more often called the Ancient and Medieval worlds). The Modern versus the Premodern world, however, remains within the context of the West. The second phase is that of the Postmodern world against the West itself (Columbus as Invader). Here the pin-up boy of Postmodernism is Nietzsche who goes far beyond the other major purveyors of bad ideas for the 20ᵗʰ Century, i.e., Marx, Freud, and Darwin, as we said in the Introduction.

Nietzsche treats us to the joyful wisdom that God is dead; that truth is an illusion; that the principle of causality is a fiction; and that science, history, law, and religion are fictions too. But as we say in the chapter on art and beauty, an earlier formidable foe of Premodernity was Machiavelli whom we and others call the founder of Modernity. His foes, as we said, were Plato, Moses, and Jesus, for the reasons we gave. Interestingly enough, these three remain the foes of Postmodernity as well, and for the same reasons: the objectivity of knowledge (Plato); the good of the moral law (Moses) and the persona of the transcendence *and* immanence of God (Jesus).

Alongside Machiavelli, we have Rousseau, the members of the Enlightenment, especially of the Radical Enlightenment (Toland, de Missy, de la

Mettrie, d'Holbach, and de Sade) as warriors on the side of Modernity and as precursors of our Four Horsemen. It is not too rash to say that the progress in science and the manifestations of art from the Renaissance forward owed little to those warriors and those horsemen. Nor is it rash to say that science, art, religion, and morality owe much to their foes who taught that knowledge and work are the ways human beings are at home in the world.

As a final word on bad ideas and the four Horsemen, we have found in our reading and in our discussions that Marxism, Freudianism, Darwinism and Nietzscheanism retain their hold on their supporters. Regardless of the fact that these doctrines have been proved false and harmful as a whole (Marxism and Freudianism) or dubious in part (Darwinism) or even self-contradictory (Nietzscheanism), and regardless of the fact that the supporters know this, they continue *to want to want* to teach them, as is the case of Marxism with the faculty at Amherst or as is the case of Freud with Harold Bloom, who *wishes* to do so as *literature*. Of course supporters of Marx and Freud are countless and not just Bloom and the faculty of Amherst. It is hard to put aside lifelong held beliefs, especially when those beliefs are presented in the name of science. To hold on to beliefs that are demonstrably false is to trash all sense of truth and objectivity. It is a sophistic dodge to say that truth and objectivity are not the game, as a Nietzschean would. To which Brooklyn Existentialists would reply: "Then tell us what the game is now and then we'll play." Otherwise, we place on the tongues of these true believers what Aristotle said of his teacher Plato but in reverse. It is not that we love "truth" less (although they do), but we love Marx, Freud, Darwin and Nietzsche more.

Bibliography

Abbagnano, Nicola. *Critical Existentialism*. Tr. & Ed. Nino Langiulli. Garden City, NY. Doubleday & Co., 1969.
_____.*La struttura dell'esistenza*. Torino: Paravia, 1939.
_____. *Possibilità e libertà*. Torino: Taylor, 1956.

Adamson, Walter. *Hegemony and Revolution: Antonio Gramsci's Political and Cultural Theory*. Berkeley: U of California Press, 1980.

Adorno, Theodor. *The Authoritarian Personality*. New York: Harper & Co. 1950.
_____. *The Philosophy of Modern Music*. Tr. Ann Mitchell and Wesley Blomster New York: The Seabury Press, 1973.

Augustine, St. *The City of God*. Tr. Marcus Dods. New York: Modern Library, 1950.
_____. *The Confessions*. Tr. Rex Warner. New York: New American Library, 1963.

Aeschliman, M.D. *The Restitution of Man: C.S. Lewis and the Case Against Scientism* (Grand Rapid, MI: W.B. Eerdmans Pub. Co., 1983.

Aquinas, Thomas. *Commentarium in Librum Dionysium De Divinis Nominis*, Cap. IV, Lectio 5 & 6 in *Opera Omnia*, Tomus XV. New York: Musurgia Publishers, 1950.
_____. *Summa Theologiae*, Pars Prima, Questio xxxix, Art. 8. Turin: Marietti, 1950.
_____. *Summa Theologiae*, Pars Prima Secundae, Questio xc, Art. 1. Turin: Marietti, 1950.

Aristotle. *Physics; Metaphysics; Nicomachean Ethics; Poetics* in *The Complete Works*, 2 vols. Princeton: Princeton U. Press, 1984.

Austin, John. *Lectures on Jurisprudence*. Selection In Stephen Presser and Jamil Zainaldin, Eds. *Law and Jurisprudence in American History*. St. Paul: West Publishing Co., 1989.

Bartel, Dennis. "Who's Who in Gurus," *Harper's Magazine. November, 1983*, pp. 50-56.

Benedict, Ruth. *Patterns of Culture*. New York: Houghton Mifflin, 1934.

Benjamin, Walter. "The Work of Art in the Age of Mechanical Reproduction," *Illuminations*. New York: Harcourt Brace & World, 1968.

Bloom, Allan. *The Closing of the American Mind*. New York: Simon & Schuster, 1987.

Boas, Franz. *The Franz Boas Reader: The Shaping of American Anthropology, 1983-1911*. Ed. George W. Stocking, Jr. Chicago: U of Chicago Press, 1974.

Brann, Eva. "Commencement Address," *St. John's College Magazine*. Annapolis, MD., July, 1974.

Bruinius, Harry. *Better for All the World: The Secret History of Forced Sterilization and America's Quest for Racial Purity*. New York: Knopf, 2005

Bullard, Sara. *Teaching Tolerance: Raising Open Minded, Empathetic Children*. New York: Doubleday, 1996.

Burke, Edmund. "A Letter to a Noble Lord" [1796] in *Harvard Classics*. New York: P.F.
Collier, 1909.
_____. *Reflections on the Revolution in France* [1796] & Paine, Thomas. *The Rights of Man* [1791-92]. Garden City, N.Y.: Doubleday Dolphin, 1961.

Burke, Richard. "Two Concepts of Liberal Education," *Academe*, 66, October, 1980, pp. 354-356.

Campbell, Joseph. *The Masks of God: Occidental Mythology*. New York: Viking Press, 1962.
_____. *The Masks of God: Oriental Mythology*. New York: Viking Press, 1962.

Cervantes, Miguel de. *Don Quijote de la Mancha*. Madrid: Saturnino, Calleja, Fernandez,
No date.

Cicero. *De Republica*. Tr. Clinton Keyes. Loeb Classical Library. Cambridge: Harvard U Press, 1953.

Crews, Frederic, Ed. *Unauthorized Freud: Doubters Confront a Legend*. New York: Viking Press, 1998.

Crick, Francis. *The Astonishing Hypothesis: The Scientific Search for the Soul*. New York: Scribner, 1994.

Cubberley, Ellwood P. *Changing Conceptions of Education*. New York: Houghton Mifflin, 1909.

Custred, Glynn. "The Forbidden Discovery of Kennewick Man," *Academic Questions*. Summer, 2000, vol. 13, No. 3, pp.12-30.

Cutler, Hugh Mercer. *Recalling Education*. Wilmington: ISI Books, 2001.

Darwin, Charles. *Autobiography* [1887]. New York: W.W. Norton, 1969.
_____. *The Descent of Man in Relation to Sex* [1871]. London: J. Murray, 1871.
_____. *The Origin of Species* [1859]. New York: The New American Library, 1958.

Dawkins, Richard. *The Blind Watchmaker: Why the Evidence of Evolution Reveals a Universe without Design*. New York: W.W. Norton & Co., 1987.
_____. *The God Delusion*. New York: Houghton Mifflin, 2006.
_____. *The Selfish Gene*. New York: Oxford U. Press, 1976.

de Tollenaere, Herman. "Heaven's Gate Mass Suicide in California: Some Early Remarks," *The Indian Skeptic*, August 15, 1997.

Dewey, John. *Dewey on Education*. Ed. Martin Dworkin. New York: Teachers College Press, 1959.

Dickerson, Tobin. *The Religious Movements Homepage Project: People's Temple* (Jonestown). http://religiosmovements.lib.virginia.edu/nrms/Jonestwn.html, Spring,
1998, modified by Rebecca Moore, 2/5/05.

The Diagnostic and Statistical Manual of the American Psychiatric Association, II Edition. Washington, D.C.: American Psychiatric Association, 1968.

Dostoyevsky, Feodor. *The Brothers Karamazov*. Tr. Constance Garnett. New York: Random House, 1950.

Eco, Umberto. *Art and Beauty in the Middle Ages*. Tr. Hugh Bredin. New Haven: Yale U. Press, 1986.

Edgerton, Robert, *Sick Societies: Challenging the Myth of Primitive Harmony.* New York: The Free Press, 1992.

Edmondson, Henry T. III. *John Dewey and the Decline of American Education.* Wilmington: ISI Books, 2006.

Egan, Kieran. *Getting It Wrong from the Beginning: Our Progressivist Inheritance from Herbert Spencer, John Dewey, and Jean Piaget.* New Haven: Yale U. Press, 2003.

Entwistle, Harold. *Antonio Gramsci: Conservative Schooling for Radical Politics.* Boston: Routledge & K. Paul, 1979.

Eysenck, H.J. *Uses and Abuses of Psychology.* Baltimore: Penguin Books Ltd., 1953.

Fontova, Humberto. *Exposing the Real Che Guevara and the Useful Idiots Who Idolize Him.* Sentinel HC, 2007.

Freeman, Derek. *Margaret Mead in Samoa.* Cambridge: Harvard U. Press, 1983.
_____. *The Fateful Hoaxing of Margaret Mead.* Boulder CO.: Westview Press, 1999.

Freud, Sigmund. *The Basic Writings of Sigmund Freud.* Tr. A.A. Brill. New York: Modern Library, 1938.
_____.*Civilization and its Discontents* [1930]. Tr. James Strachey. New York: W.W. Norton & Co: 1961.
_____.*A General Introduction to Psychoanalysis* [1920]. Tr. Joan Riviere. Garden City, N.Y.: Doubleday Permabooks, 1953.
_____. *Moses and Monotheism* [1939]. Tr. Katherine Jones. New York: Vintage Books, 1955.

Frick, William. *Humanistic Psychology: Conversations with Abraham Maslow, Gardner Murphy and Carl Rogers.* Bristol, Indiana: Wyndham Hall Press, 1971.

Friedan, Betty. *The Feminine Mystique.* New York: W. W. Norton, 1963.

Fromm, Erich. *Escape From Freedom.* New York: Holt, Rinehart and Winston, 1941.
_____. *The Dogma of Christ.* New York: Holt, Rinehart and Winston, 1963.

Futuyma, Douglas. *Evolution.* Sunderland, MA: Sinnauer Associates, 2005.

Gardiner, Ann Barbeau. Review of Christine Rosen's *Preaching Eugenics*. *New Oxford Review*, October 2006, pp. 42-45.

Gardner, Martin. "A Skeptical Look at Karl Popper," *Are Universes Thicker than Blackberries?* New York: W.W. Norton, 2003.

Gatto, John Taylor. *The Underground History of American Education*. New York: Oxford Village Press, 2000/2001.

Gay, Peter. *Freud: A Life for Our Time*. New York: Simon Schuster, 1988.

Goethe, Johann Wolfgang von. *Faust, Parts I & II*. Tr. Albert Latham. New York: E.P. Dutton & Co., 1908.

Goldberg, Steven. *When Wish Replaces Thought*. Buffalo: Prometheus Books, 1991.

Gospel of *Matthew*; Gospel of *John*; *Apocalypse. New Testament*. Challoner-Douay Rheims Version [1750]. New York: Confraternity of Christian Doctrine, 1941.

Gottfried, Paul. *Multiculturalism and the Politics of Guilt: Towards a Secular Theocracy*. Columbia, Mo: U. of Missouri Press, 2002.
_____. *The Strange Death of Marxism*. Columbia, Mo: U. of Missouri Press, 2005.

Gould, Stephen Jay. "Abscheurlich! Atrocious!" *Natural History*, March, 2000, pp. 42-49.
_____. "Evolution as Fact and Theory," *Hen's Teeth and Horse's Toes*. New York: W.W. Norton & Co., 1994.
_____. *The Structure of Evolutionary Theory*. Cambridge: Harvard U. Press, 2002.

Gramsci, Antonio. "In Search of Educational Principles." Tr. Quintin Hoare. *New Left Review*, No. 32, July-August, 1965, pp. 55-62.
_____. *Letters from Prison*. Tr. Lynne Lawner. New York: Harper & Row, 1973.
_____. *The Modern Prince and Other Writings*. London: Lawrence and Wishart, 1957.
_____. *Prison Notebooks*. Tr. Joseph Buttigieg and Antonio Callari. New York: Columbia U. Press, 1992.

Grant, Robert. *Gnosticism and Early Christianity*. New York: Harper Torchbooks, 1966.

Hadden, Jeffrey & Saliba, John. *The Religious Movements Homepage Project: Heaven's Gate.* http: // religiousmovements.lib.virginia.edu/nrms/hgprofile.html,2005.

Hall, G. Stanley. *Educational Problems.* 2 vols. New York: Houghton Mifflin, 1911.

Heidegger, Martin. *Being and Time.* Tr. John Macquarrie and Edward Robinson [A Translation of *Zein Und Zeit,* 1927] New York: Harper & Row, 1962.
_____."The Origin of the Work of Art," in *Philosophies of Art and Beauty,* Eds. Albert Hofstadter and Richard Kuhns. New York: Modern Library, 1964.

Hirsch, E.D. Jr. *The Schools We Need: Why We Don't Have Them.* New York: Doubleday, 1996.

Holmes, Oliver Wendell Jr. "The Path of the Law," in Stephen Presser and Jamil Zainaldin, Eds. *Law and Jurisprudence in American History.* St. Paul: West Publishing Co., 1989.

Howard, Philip K. *The Death of Common Sense: How Law is Suffocating America.* NewYork: Random House, 1995.

Jacob, Margaret. *The Radical Enlightenment: Pantheists, Freemasons and Republicans.* London: Allen & Unwin, 1981.

John Paul II, Pope. *Fides et Ratio.* Rome: Vatican, 1998.

Johnson, Paul. *Intellectuals.* New York: Harper & Row, 1988.

Jonas, Hans. *The Gnostic Religion.* Boston: Beacon Press, 1963.

Jones, E. Michael. *Degenerate Moderns.* San Francisco: Ignatius Press, 1993.
_____. *Dionysos Rising.* San Francisco: Ignatius Press, 1994.
_____. *Living Machines.* San Francisco: Ignatius Press, 1995.

Joseph, Sister Miriam. *The Trivium: The Liberal Arts of Logic, Grammar, and Rhetoric.* Philadelphia: Paul Dry, 2002.

Kelsen, Hans. *General Theory of Law and State.* Cambridge: Harvard U. Press, 1945.

Kilpatrick, William Heard. *Foundations of Method: Informal Talks on Teaching.* New York: Macmillan, 1925.

Kilpatrick, William K. *Psychological Seduction: the Failure of Modern Psychology*. Nashville: Thomas Nelson, 1983.

_____.*Why Johnny Can't Tell Right from Wrong: Moral Illiteracy and the Case for Character Education*. New York: Simon & Schuster, 1992.

Kimball, Roger. *The Long March: How the Cultural Revolution Changed America*. San Francisco: Encounter Books, 2000.

Kinsey, Alfred. *Sexual Behavior in the Human Female*. Philadelphia: W.B. Saunder, Co.,
1953.

_____. *Sexual Behavior in the Human Male*. Philadelphia: W.B. Saunder, Co., 1948.

Koestler, Arthur. *The Sleepwalkers*. New York: Macmillan, 1959.

Kramer, Yale. "Freud and the Culture Wars," *The Public Interest*, vol. 124, Summer, 1996, pp. 37-51.

Langiulli, Nino, Ed. *European Existentialism*. New Brunswick: Transaction Press, 1997.

_____." A Liberal Education: Knowing What to Resist," *Academic Questions*, Summer, 2000, Vol. 13. No. 3, pp. 39-45.

Le Corbusier. *Towards a New Architecture*. Tr. Frederick Etchells. London: The Architectural Press, 1927.

Lombardo, Paul. "Eugenic Sterilization Laws," *Image Archive on the American Eugenics Movement*. Cold Spring Harbor Laboratory, Date Unavailable.

Lukács, Georg. *Marxism and Human Liberation*. Ed. E. San Juan, Jr. New York: Delta Books, 1973.

Machiavelli, Niccolò. *Il Principe* [1532]. Milano: Mondadori, 1994.

_____. *The Prince*. Tr. Thomas Bergin. New York: Appleton Century Crofts, 1947.

_____. *The Prince*. Tr. David Wooton. Indianapolis: Hackett, 1995.

Marcuse, Herbert. *Eros and Civilization: A Philosophical Inquiry into Freud*. Boston: The Beacon Press, 1955.

_____. *One Dimensional Man*. Boston: the Beacon Press, 1964.

Marlowe, Christopher. *The Tragical History of Dr. Faustus*. New York: Appleton Century Crofts, 1950.

Marx, Karl. *The German Ideology*. Selections in Eugene Kamenka, Ed. *The Portable Karl Marx*. New York: Viking Penguin, 1983.
_____.*The Grundrisse*. Ed. & Tr. David Mc Lellan. New York: Harper & Row, 1971.
_____. *Theses on Feuerbach*. in Loyd Easton and Kurt Guddat, Eds. & Trs. *Writings of the Young Marx on Philosophy and Society*. New York: Doubleday Anchor Books, 1967.

Maslow, Abraham. *Motivation and Personality*. New York: Harper & Co., 1954.
_____. *Towards a Psychology of Being*. New York: John Wiley & Sons, 1962.

Mayr, Ernst. *The Growth of Biological Thought*. Cambridge: Harvard U. Press, 1982.

Mead, Margaret. *Coming of Age in Samoa*. New York: William Morrow, 1928.
_____. *Growing Up in new Guinea*. New York: William Morrow, 1930.
_____. *Sex and Temperament in Three Primitive Societies*. New York: William Morrow, 1935.

Milton, Joyce. *Malpsychia: Humanistic Psychology and its Discontents*. San Francisco: Encounter books, 2002.

Muggeridge, Ann Roche. *The Desolate City: Revolution in the Catholic Church*. New York: Harper Collins, 1986. Paper ed. 1990.

Nietzsche, Friedrich. *The Birth of Tragedy*[1872] and *The Genealogy of Morals* [1887]. Tr. Francis Golffing. Garden City, NY: Doubleday & Co., 1956.
_____."Truth and Falsity in the Ultramoral Sense" [1872] in Nino Langiulli, ed.
European Existentialism. New Brunswick: Transaction Publishers, 1997.
_____. *The Will To Power*. Tr. W. Kaufmann & H.J. Hollingdale. New York: Random House, 1967.

Pagels, Elaine. *The Gnostic Gospels*. New York: Vintage Books, 1981.

Plato. *Apology; Republic; Theaetetus; Timaeus* in *The Collected Dialogues*. Eds. Edith Hamilton and Huntington Cairns. New York: Pantheon, 1961.

Popper, Karl. *Conjectures and Refutations: The Growth of Scientific Knowledge.* New York: Harper & Row, 1963.
_____. *The Logic of Scientific Discovery.* London: Hutchinson & Co., 1959.

Postman, Neil. *Amusing Ourselves to Death: Public Discourse in the Age of Show Business.* New York: Viking Penguin, 1985.

Powell, S.J., John. *The John Powell Calendar.* Allen, Texas: Argus Communications, 1981.

Pritchett, C. Herman. *The American Constitution,* 3rd Edition. New York: McGraw Hill,
1977.

Prosser, Charles. *Secondary Education and Life.* Cambridge: Harvard U. Press, 1939.

Ravitch, Diane. *The Language Police: How Pressure Groups Restrict What Students Learn.* New York: Knopf, 2003.
_____. *Left Back.* New York: Simon & Schuster, 2000.

Reich, Wilhelm. *Mass Psychology of Fascism.* New York Orgone Institute Press, 1946.
_____. *The Sexual Revolution* [a translation of Die *Sexualität im Kulturkamp* (1936)] New York: Orgone Institute Press, 1945.

Reisman, Judith. *Kinsey: Crimes and Consequences. The Red Queen and the Grand Scheme.* Crestwood, Ky.: Institute for Media Education, 1998.
_____. et al. *Kinsey, Sex and Fraud: The Indoctrination of a People.* Vital Issues Press, 1990.

Rieff, Philip. *My Life Among the Deathworks.* Charlottesville: U. of Virginia Press, 2006.
_____. *The Triumph of the Therapeutic.* New York: Harper & Row, 1966.

Roach, Mary. *Spook: Science Tackles the Afterlife.* New York: W.W. Norton & Co., 2005.

Rogers, Carl. *On Becoming a Person: A Therapist's View of Psychotherapy.* Boston: Houghton Mifflin, 1961.
_____. "This is Me." in *The Carl Rogers Reader.* Ed. Howard Kirschenbaum and Valerie Land Henderson. Boston: Houghton Mifflin, 1989.

Rose, Mike. "United We Stand: Schools Deliver Crucial Message on Tolerance," *The American Teacher*. Washington D.C., Dec. 2001-Jan. 2002.

Sartre, Jean-Paul. *The Critique of the Dialectical Reason* [1960]. Tr. Alan Sheridan-Smith. Ed. Jonathan Rèe. Atlantic Highlands, N.J: Humanities Press, 1976.
_____. "Existentialism is a Humanism," [1946]. Tr. Philip Mairet [1948] in *European Existentialism*. Ed. Nino Langiulli. New Brunswick. Transaction Press, 1997.

Sayre, Anne. *Rosalind Franklin and DNA*. New York: W. W. Norton, 1975.

Scruton, Roger. *The Aesthetic Understanding*. South Bend: St. Augustine's Press, 1998.
_____. *The West and the Rest: Globalization and the Terrorist Threat*. Wilmington: ISI Books, 2002.

Shakespeare, William. *As You Like It; Hamlet; Henry VI, Part II* in *Complete Works*. London: Oxford U. Press, 1905.

Skell, Philip S. "Why Do We Invoke Darwin?" *The Scientist*, August 29, 2005, p. 10.

Skinner, B.F. *Beyond Freedom and Dignity*. New York: Knopf, 1971.
_____. *Science and Human Behavior*. New York: Macmillan, 1953.

Slade, Francis. "On the Ontological Priority of Ends and its Relevance to the Narrative Arts," *Beauty, Art, and the Polis*. Ed. Alice Ramos. American Maritain Association, Washington, D.C.: The Catholic University Press, 2004.

Smolin, Lee. *The Trouble with Physics: The Rise of String Theory, the Fall of a Science and What Comes Next*. New York: Houghton Mifflin, 2006.

Sommers, Christina. "Hard Line Feminists Guilty of Ms.-Representation," *Wall Street Journal*, 11/17/91. Editorial page.

Sowell, Thomas. *Marxism: Philosophy and Economics*. New York: William Morrow, 1985.
Spencer, Herbert. *Principles of Biology*. New York: D. Appleton & Co., 1880.

Steichen, Donna. *Ungodly Rage*. San Francisco: Ignatius Press, 1991.

Stern-La Rosa, Caryl & Bettman, Ellen Hoffmeir. Hate Hurts: *How Children Learn and Unlearn Prejudice*. New York: Scholastic, 2000.

Stove, David. *Against the Idols of the Age*. New Brunswick: Transaction Press, 1999.

Strauss, Leo. *"Jerusalem and Athens: Some Preliminary Reflections,"* The City College Papers, 6. New York: City University of New York, 1967, pp. 3-28.
_____. *Natural Right and History.* Chicago: U. of Chicago Press, 1953.
_____. *Thoughts on Machiavelli.* Glencoe, Illinois: The Free Press, 1958.

Swales, Peter. "Freud, Minna Bernays, and the Conquest of Rome," *New American Review*1, Spring/Summer, 1982, pp. 1-23.

Swift, Jonathan. *The Battle of the Books* [1710] in *Selected Prose & Poetry.* New York: Holt, Rinehart and Winston, 1959.

Terman, Lewis, et al. *Intelligence Tests and School Reorganization.* Yonkers, NY: World Book, 1923.

Thorndike, Edward L. *Educational Psychology: Briefer Course.* New York: Teachers College Press, 1914.

Thornton, Bruce. *Plagues of the Mind. The New Epidemic of False Knowledge.* Wilmington: ISI Books, 1999.

Venturi, Robert. *Complexity and Contradiction in Architecture.* Garden City, NY: Doubleday & Co., 1966.

Voegelin, Eric. *Science, Politics and Gnosticism.* Chicago: Regnery, 1968.

Watson, James & Crick, Francis. *The Structure of DNA.* Cold Spring Harbor, NY: Biological Laboratory, 1953.

Watts, Alan. *The Way of Zen.* New York: Vintage Books, 1957.

Wellerstein, Alex. "Harry Laughlin's Model Sterilization Law." http://www.people. fas.harvard.edu/~wellerst/Laughlin/,2006.

Wells, Jonathan. *Icons of Evolution: Science or Myth.* Washington, D.C.: Regnery, 2000.

_____. *The Politically Incorrect Guide to Darwinism and Intelligent Design.* Washington, D.C.: Regnery, 2006.

Wilson, Edward O. *Sociobiology; The New Synthesis.* Cambridge: Harvard U. Press, 1975.

Woit, Peter. *Not Even Wrong: The Failure of String Theory and the Search for Unity in Physical Law*. New York: Basic Books, 2006.

Wolfe, Tom. *From Bauhaus to Our House*. New York: McGraw Hill, 1981.
_____.*The Painted Word*. New York: Farrar Straus & Giroux, 1975.
_____. "The Worship of Art." *Harper's* Magazine, October, 1984, pp. 61-68.

A

Abbot, Jack Henry 139
Abraham 103, 106
Abstract Expressionism 175
Abstractionism 175
Abzug, Bella 66
Achilles 163
Adam, Ansel 186
Adorno, Theodor 63, 180, 181
affirmative action 13 145
Alexander 162, 185
Alice in Wonderland Jurisprudence 129
Alpert, Richard (see also Baba Ram Das)
114
American Idol 156
American tort jurisprudence 143
Amherst 15
Anaxagoras 88, 99
Apollo 19
Applewhite, Marshall 111, 112
Archaeopteryx 18
Aristarchus of Samos 89
Aristotle 19, 20, 39, 77, 88, 92, 126,
149, 164, 174
Aristotle's Metaphysics 70
Art 170, 183
Astarte 104
Atomists 78
Attica Prison riot of 1970 139
Augustine 99
Austin, John 128, 137
Avedon, Richard 186
Avicenna 81

B

Baal 104
Baba Ram Das (see also Richard Alpert)
114
Bach, Johan Sebastian 153, 182
Bacon, Francis 167
Bartok, Bela 182

Bauhaus 183, 196
Beat 65
Beatles, The 39, 113
beauty 180, 195
Beethoven, Ludwig van 182
Beethoven's Ninth Symphony
151
Benedict, Ruth 64, 66, 67, 68,
69, 70
Benedictines 78
Benjamin, Walter 142
Berg, Alban 182
Bergman, Ingmar 187
Berkely, Busby 180
Bernanos, Georges 16
Besant, Annie 112
Black, Hugo 66
Blavatsky, Madame 112
Bloom, Allan 155 197
Bloom, Harold 16, 197
Bohr, Neils 173
Bolling v. Sharpe 145
Bosch, Hieronymus 147
Bork, Robert 120
Brancusi, Constantin 175, 176
Brann, Eva 48
Braque, Georges 175
Bresson-Cartier, Henri 186
*Brown v. Board of Education of
Topeka* (1954) 66, 145
Buck, Carrie 132, 133, 134
Buck v. Bell 131
Buehrig, Gordon 181
Buonarroti, Michelangelo 149,
153, 187
Burke, Edmund 132, 139
Burns, Ken 32
Burroughs, William S. 64
busing 28

C

Caesar 163